Don't Move to Asheville

A Ruthlessly Honest Guide That Will Ruin Everywhere Else

PAUL WILCZYNSKI

Published by TheSeniorTechie Press, Asheville, North Carolina

Every fact in this book was verified to the best of the author's ability at the time of writing. Asheville changes faster than a weather system coming over the Black Mountains. Some details—prices, business hours, development timelines, political winds—will have shifted by the time you read this. The author apologizes for nothing except the errors.

Print ISBN: 979-8-9955017-0-1
eBook ISBN: 979-8-9955017-1-8
Library of Congress Control Number: 2026908269

First Edition, 2026

Interior design and layout by Andrea Kulish Wilhelm

Front cover design concept by Paul Wilczynski and Andrea Kulish Wilhelm; some imagery created with assistance from generative tools.

Illustration credits: p. 51 Bogdan/stock.adobe.com; p. 73 mrvect02/stock.adobe.com; p. 97 Vladislav/stock. adobe.com; p. 125 Khoirul/stock.adobe.com; p. 153 MDShuvo/stock.adobe.com and Ejiii/stock.adobe.com; p. 229 DesignThatMatters//stock.adobe.com

https://www.DontMoveToAsheville.com

For Joan.

We left Boston for the warmth. We left Charleston for the cool. We found Asheville. I am the luckiest of people.

She has been my companion in every mile of it. The geography changes. The company never has.

Thirty years. Still going.

TABLE OF CONTENTS

CHAPTER ONE

DON'T MOVE HERE
IF YOU LIKE BORING FOOD

The food will ruin you.

Let's get this out of the way right now. If you move to Asheville, North Carolina, you will never again be fully satisfied eating anywhere else. That's not a threat. It's an inevitability, the kind that sneaks up on you around month four, when you find yourself in some other perfectly decent American city, staring at a menu that lists nothing about where the food came from, and you feel a small, specific sense of loss you did not see coming.

You had no idea this would happen to you. Nobody warned you. You thought it was just a cute mountain town with nice breweries. You had been told, correctly, that the cost of living was reasonable and the scenery was extraordinary and the people were interesting.

You were not told about the food. Nobody warns you about the food.

You were wrong.

Asheville, with a population of roughly 95,000 people, has assembled a food scene that would be considered exceptional in cities five or ten times its size. The James Beard Foundation noticed. Michelin noticed. The New York Times noticed years ago. Travel + Leisure noticed. Yelp no ticed. Everyone has noticed except, somehow, the people who still think of it as a quirky little arts town in the hills.

It is a quirky arts town in the hills. It is also, undeniably, a serious food city. Both things are equally true, which is part of what makes it so disorienting.

The Scale of the Problem

Most American cities of Asheville's size have a handful of decent local restaurants, a middling chain situation, and maybe one or two places genuinely worth driving to. Asheville has over 250 independent restaurants. The Chamber of Commerce calls that number deliberately conservative.

Researchers at Georgia Tech built something called a Restaurant Chaininess Map, which sounds like the name of a scientific instrument designed specifically to measure how bad a city's food situation has gotten. The idea is straightforward. Every restaurant in America gets a score based on how many locations it has. A one-of-a-kind taco truck scores close to 1. A regional chain with 50 locations scores higher. McDonald's, with thousands of outlets blanketing the country, scores over 10,000.

Cities full of chains end up with a high average. Cities full of genuine independents score low. Asheville scores low. What this means, practically, is that there is no safe Applebee's to retreat to when you're tired and just want something predictable. You are going to make a real decision every single time.

Consider yourself warned.

When the Washington Post reported on the data in 2022, Asheville ranked as one of the least chain-dominated food cities in the country. About 28 percent of its restaurants are chains. The other 72 percent exist only here — you will not find them anywhere else, because there is nowhere else to find them.

This is, as food problems go, among the worst kinds to have.

What that means in practice is that every time you go out to eat, you're making an actual decision. There is no defaulting to something familiar because you're tired. Routine dining does not exist here. You will find yourself spending ten minutes reading menus online before a Tuesday night dinner, not because you're indecisive, but because there are genuinely too many excellent options.

This is, objectively, a problem.

At first, this feels exciting. After about six months, it starts to feel like a part-time job. You will maintain a running list of places you haven't tried yet. The list will grow faster than you can work through it, because new restaurants keep opening and because Asheville is the kind of city that attracts the kind of people who open restaurants worth going to. The list does not get shorter. You will make peace with this, eventually, but not for a while.

Oscar Wong and the Basement That Changed Everything

Before we talk food, we have to talk beer, because the two are inseparable in Asheville, and because the whole problem starts in a basement on Biltmore Avenue in 1994. If you want someone to blame for what Asheville became, Oscar Wong is your man.

Oscar Wong was a retired civil engineer. He was born in Jamaica, came to the United States to study at the University of Notre Dame, built a successful engineering firm, sold it, and retired at a relatively young age. He had been homebrewing beer since college. He had spent years vacationing in Asheville with his family, loved the mountains, loved the independent-minded culture, and had a specific vision for what his second career would look like.

A reasonable person might have taken up golf. Oscar Wong did not take up golf.

On April 21, 1994, Wong opened Highland Brewing Company in a rented basement beneath what is now Barley's Taproom and Pizzeria on Biltmore Avenue. It was the first legal craft brewery in Asheville since Prohibition. He brewed his first batches on repurposed dairy equipment he had refitted himself. He sold beer out of that basement for thirteen years.

This was the original sin. One retired engineer, a homebrew habit, some secondhand dairy tanks, and now you cannot visit Asheville without developing opinions about dry-hopping.

Highland grew. Green Man Brewing followed, then Asheville Brewing Company, then others. From 2011 to 2014, the number of craft breweries in the area nearly doubled. The South Slope neighborhood — a stretch of old warehouses and brick buildings packed close together just south of downtown — became home to nine breweries within less than a mile of each other. National publications started paying attention.

In 2009, craft beer writer Charlie Papazian ran an annual poll asking readers to vote for Beer City USA. Asheville took the title that first year, tied with Portland. Then won outright the following year. Then the year after that. Then tied again for first. Four consecutive years at the top of the poll, which is the kind of thing that eventually stops being a coincidence.

The Beer City USA designation caught the attention of Sierra Nevada, one of the country's most respected craft brewers. They opened an East Coast campus in Mills River, just outside Asheville, in 2014. New Belgium Brewing — at the time the fourth-largest craft brewer in the nation — opened its East Coast brewery near Asheville's River

Arts District in 2016. The Asheville Area Chamber of Commerce now states flatly that Asheville has more craft breweries per capita than any other city in the United States.

The arrival of Sierra Nevada and New Belgium was significant beyond the obvious. When breweries of that scale choose a location for a second campus, they are not choosing arbitrarily. They are choosing a city with an existing culture of serious beer drinkers, a local supply chain of quality ingredients, and a community of smaller producers who have already trained the regional palate. Asheville had all three. The national brands did not create the beer culture here. They showed up because it already existed and decided they wanted to be part of it.

Today, more than 20 breweries pour over 200 local craft beers on tap on any given day. That includes tiny taproom nano-breweries, the South Slope's cluster of mid-size operations, and Highland's forty-acre campus, now led by Wong's daughter Leah Wong Ashburn, who has run the brewery since 2015.

The Wedge Brewing Company is a useful illustration of how this works in practice. Tim Schaller opened it in May 2008 in the River Arts District, in a 1916 building that had previously been an agricultural co-op, a medical textile company, and eventually a sculptor's studio complex. Carl Melissas, who had been homebrewing competitively and put in two years at Green Man before teaming up with Schaller, became the brewer. The Iron Rail IPA — named for the railroad tracks that defined the neighborhood long before anyone thought to put a beer garden next to them — won Best Beer in Asheville two years running.

The Wedge made a deliberate decision early on to sell almost entirely on-premises, cutting most outside distribution to keep the beer fresh and the taproom full. You cannot pick up a six-pack at the grocery store. You have to go there. The brewery now operates two locations, both in the RAD: the original at 37 Paynes Way, where a steel dinosaur skeleton peers down at the beer garden from above the entrance with the equanimity of something that has seen real estate prices come and go, and a second at 5 Foundy Street, built inside a former leather tannery that dates to 1898. Asheville understood the on-premises model immediately. The beer garden fills up on Thursday afternoons with a clientele that runs from painters in work clothes to professionals who drove across town specifically.

Hurricane Helene flooded the Foundy Street location in September 2024. The brewery didn't close permanently. Schaller kept staff employed through the cleanup, the beer garden was rebuilt, new trees went in, and the taproom reopened in October 2025 with sixteen beers on tap. In a neighborhood still accounting for what it lost, that is not a small thing.

Oscar Wong passed away in May 2025, at the age of 84. The city of Asheville and Buncombe County had declared May 16 as Oscar Wong Day in 2023. That same year, the governor of North Carolina awarded him the Order of the Long Leaf Pine, the state's highest civilian honor. There is a bronze plaque on the sidewalk outside Barley's Taproom marking the basement where all of it started.

The thing about Oscar Wong is that his story is also Asheville's story. A person with skill and vision and enough independence to follow an unconventional idea found in Asheville the conditions that made the idea work. He was not the last person this would happen to. He was the first.

If you move to Asheville, you will walk past that plaque regularly. You will probably stop and look at it. You will almost certainly be holding a pint of something excellent at the time, which is exactly as it should be, and exactly the problem.

What James Beard Actually Means

The James Beard Foundation Awards are the most prestigious recognition in American culinary life. Winning one is a significant milestone for any restaurant or chef. Winning two in the same night, in the same small city, for the first time in that city's history, is something else entirely.

That's what happened in June 2022, at the James Beard Awards ceremony held at the Chicago Lyric Opera.

Chai Pani won Outstanding Restaurant — the top restaurant award the Foundation gives. Meherwan and Molly Irani opened it in downtown Asheville in 2009 as an Indian street food restaurant, scrappy and colorful and loud, funded by family and friends. It ran out of food on opening day. In 2022, it beat out formal restaurants in major cities for the most prestigious restaurant award in the country. In May 2024, the restaurant moved to a larger space at 32 Banks Avenue in the South Slope, taking over the former Buxton Hall Barbecue building — a former roller-skating rink that once served Asheville's Black community. Irani's restaurant group now includes Botiwalla, a fast-casual Indian street grill with multiple locations across the South, and Spicewalla, a small-batch spice brand that started as a kitchen supply operation and ended up on Oprah's Favorite Things list.

Spicewalla deserves a moment. Irani started it to supply fresh, high-quality spices to his own kitchens, because the commercially available options were not good enough. Other chefs started asking for it. He launched a retail line in the summer of 2019. Months later, Oprah put the 18-spice pack on her annual Favorite Things list. The company built an e-commerce platform in thirty days. When the pandemic hit and restaurant revenue collapsed, Spicewalla revenue quadrupled. The spice brand built in Asheville to supply one restaurant group now ships over 250 products to home cooks and professional kitchens across the country. All of it, like almost everything in this chapter, started with someone deciding that Asheville was the right place to do something seriously.

Cúrate won Outstanding Hospitality that same night. Katie Button and Felix Meana opened the Spanish tapas restaurant on Biltmore Avenue in 2011. The Hospitality award recognizes service culture and the sustainable workforce a restaurant creates. Winning it the same night Chai Pani won Outstanding Restaurant meant two Asheville restaurants took two of the Foundation's top prizes in a single evening.

Two restaurants. Two top awards. Same night.

This does not happen to cities of 95,000 people.

For what it's worth: Chai Pani's bhel puri costs less than ten dollars. The sloppy jai runs around thirteen. This is not fine dining in the traditional sense. The restaurant is casual, colorful, and loud in the best way, and the fact that it beat formal restaurants in major cities for Outstanding Restaurant says something specific about what that award actually measures: the total experience, the food, the culture, the way a place exists in its city.

Cúrate tells the same kind of story. Button found Asheville partly by stopping at the North Asheville Tailgate Market on a spring day and being floored by the density and quality of what local farmers were selling. She built a Spanish tapas concept on those local ingredients alongside imported Spanish staples. The two things coexist without contradiction.

That's an Asheville thing.

The 2025 Wave and the Michelin Moment

The 2022 wins were not a fluke. Three years later, in 2025, Asheville had another exceptional year in national culinary recognition. And then one more thing happened that nobody in a city of 95,000 people has any right to expect.

Michelin showed up.

In November 2025, the MICHELIN Guide released its inaugural American South edition, covering restaurants across six states. Asheville landed 15 recognitions — the most of any city in North Carolina. Luminosa, an Italian-American restaurant inside the Flat Iron Hotel that draws almost entirely on Western North Carolina farms and producers, earned a MICHELIN Green Star for sustainability. Only three restaurants in the entire American South received that distinction. Luminosa also earned a Bib Gourmand, the designation Michelin uses for exceptional food at a moderate price.

Little Chango, a South Slope arepa restaurant led by Chef Iris Rodriguez, also earned a Bib Gourmand. So did Mother, a neighborhood cafe and wine bar built around naturally leavened bread. Twelve more Asheville restaurants appeared on the Recommended list, including Cúrate, Good Hot Fish, Leo's House of Thirst, Sunny Point Cafe, and The Admiral.

The Recommended designation, for the uninitiated, means a tire company based in France has decided your neighborhood restaurant is worth a detour. The practical effect, for anyone who actually lives in Asheville, is that twelve more places you used to walk into on a Wednesday now have a line.

You are welcome.

Also in 2025, three Asheville chefs earned James Beard recognition. William Dissen of The Market Place was nominated for Outstanding Chef. Silver Iocovozzi of Neng Jr's was a finalist for Best Chef: Southeast — having already been named Food and Wine's Best New Chef in 2024. Ashleigh Shanti of Good Hot Fish was a semifinalist for Best Chef: Southeast. Leo's House of Thirst received a nomination for Outstanding Wine and Other Beverages Program, the same year it appeared on the Michelin Recommended list.

A city of 95,000 people. One Michelin Green Star. Multiple Bib Gourmands. Multiple Michelin recommended restaurants. James Beard nominations spanning multiple years. Food and Wine's Best New Chef. All of this, simultaneously, in a mountain city where you moved because you heard the cost of living was reasonable.

"Reasonable cost of living" and "fifteen Michelin-recognized restaurants within walking distance" are fundamentally incompatible with maintaining a sensible budget. You will discover this around month six.

The city was also recognized as having more Michelin-recognized restaurants than any other city in North Carolina. In an inaugural year for the regional guide, that is not a small thing.

William Dissen and Forty-Six Years of Farm-to-Table

If there is one person who embodies the intersection of Asheville's food culture, its agricultural connections, and its national recognition, it is William Dissen of The Market Place.

The Market Place opened in 1979. It is Asheville's original farm-to-table restaurant, which matters because the farm-to-table movement was not a named thing yet in 1979. The restaurant was sourcing from local farms before doing so was fashionable, before it was a marketing angle, before anyone had invented language for it.

Dissen did not open The Market Place. He discovered it.

He was living in Charleston, South Carolina, came to Asheville for a concert at the LEAF Festival, stopped at an Earth Fare market, and picked up a copy of the Appalachian Sustainable Agriculture Project's Local Food Guide. He spent the next week calling a real estate agent. The agent mentioned an established restaurant for sale. He met the previous owner, Mark Rosenstein, who had opened the place in 1979. In 2009, Dissen bought it.

He has since been nominated for Outstanding Chef by the James Beard Foundation, and the restaurant was a semi-finalist for Outstanding Restaurant. The Market Place's sourcing philosophy is literal: ingredients from within 100 miles, from farms Dissen can name in conversation, with those farm names posted on a sign in the dining room. Fortune Magazine named him Green Chef of the Year two years running.

Then there is the television moment. Gordon Ramsay came to Western North Carolina to film an episode of National Geographic's "Gordon Ramsay: Uncharted." He toured the mountains and rivers with Dissen, learned about heirloom ingredients and Appalachian foodways, and at the end of a head-to-head cook-off, lost. Ramsay had never lost in three seasons of the show. He called Dissen the most sustainable chef on the planet. The judges — local people Ramsay had spent the week with — gave the win to the local guy.

When Dissen talks about why he cooks this way, he traces it to culinary school. He was told that to be the best chef, you use the best ingredients. Most of his classmates heard foie gras and truffles and caviar. He heard the Appalachian farmers his grandmother worked with: the freshness of ingredients that hadn't traveled a thousand miles, the specificity of a region's soil and season expressed through what grows in it.

This is the foundation of what The Market Place does, and

it is also a description of what Asheville's best restaurants have in common. They are not trying to import a culinary tradition from somewhere else. They are trying to understand what grows here, who grows it, and how to translate that into something worth eating. The result, over 46 years at The Market Place and across dozens of other restaurants, is a food culture with a genuine sense of place. That is rarer than it sounds.

Neng Jr's and What Happens When a City Attracts This Kind of Chef

Silver Iocovozzi grew up in a Filipino family and spent years cooking in various kitchens, including at Chai Pani, before opening Neng Jr's in West Asheville in the summer of 2022. The restaurant has 17 seats. It is small by any measure.

The cuisine is Filipino-American with deep Appalachian roots, which sounds like it might require explanation but doesn't, really, once you eat there. Iocovozzi picks from local farms, forages when possible, and builds the menu around what the region produces. Duck adobo. Ice cream made with sharp cheddar and mimolette. Kinilaw, a raw seafood preparation. Lumpia. Brunswick stew. The menu shifts constantly based on what's available.

Eating at Neng Jr's is less like going to a restaurant and more like being handed a very specific argument about what food can be. The portions are not large. The room is close and warm. The menu has no obvious throughline until it does, suddenly, because the throughline is the region itself — its farms, its foraged ingredients, its specific growing season. A dish made with ramps in spring will not be on the menu in summer. What replaces it will be equally specific, equally rooted, and equally worth planning around.

Two years after opening, Iocovozzi was named Food and Wine's Best New Chef for 2024. In 2025, Neng Jr's was a

James Beard finalist for Best Chef: Southeast. Reservations are booked out a month in advance. There are mid-size conference rooms in American office buildings with more capacity.

If you want to eat at Neng Jr's, plan accordingly. Treat it like a dental procedure. This is not a complaint. It is a warning.

Iocovozzi has said that Appalachian food has profoundly influenced the cooking because it shares a sensibility with Filipino food: working with what you have, preservation, making something delicious from ingredients that don't announce themselves. The two traditions sit comfortably together in the same kitchen because they come from the same place philosophically, even if geographically they could not be more different. It is food that takes resourcefulness seriously, that treats limitations as a design constraint rather than an obstacle. Asheville, with its specific growing season, its specific farms, its specific landscape, provides exactly those constraints.

The fact that Iocovozzi chose to open here, rather than in New York or Los Angeles or Chicago, is worth sitting with. Asheville is not the obvious choice for a chef at this level. And yet it keeps being the choice. Meherwan Irani chose it in 2009. Katie Button chose it in 2011. Silver Iocovozzi chose it in 2022. Ashleigh Shanti, whose restaurant Good Hot Fish draws on the heritage of African American seafood traditions, chose it.

The city pulls this caliber of person in a way that larger markets cannot fully explain. Part of the answer is practical: cost of living is lower, real estate for restaurant space is more accessible, and the customer base, though smaller, is unusually engaged. Part of the answer is cultural: Asheville has a long-established identity as a place that takes independent creative work seriously, and that reputation reaches people in kitchens in other cities. But part of the answer is probably just that Asheville keeps producing the conditions under which serious cooking thrives, and word has gotten around.

The Farms Are Not a Backdrop. They're the Point.

You cannot fully understand why Asheville's restaurants are the way they are without understanding the agricultural landscape wrapped around them. This is inconvenient, because it means the problem goes deeper than the restaurants.

Western North Carolina is surrounded by some of the most productive small-farm land in the eastern United States. The Southern Appalachians create a series of microclimates, valleys, and elevations that support an unusually wide range of crops and livestock. Cooler temperatures extend the growing season for crops that would bolt in summer heat elsewhere. Heirloom vegetables that would struggle in flatter farmland thrive here. Heritage-breed animals are well-suited to the terrain.

The combination of elevation, rainfall, and soil produces ingredients with flavor profiles that are genuinely distinct. That is a polite way of saying that once you have eaten an Asheville-area strawberry in May, the ones anywhere else will seem like a different fruit. A worse fruit. A fruit that has given up.

This is not a reversible condition.

Hickory Nut Gap Farm in Fairview has been part of the region's agricultural fabric since 1916, when Jim and Elizabeth McClure purchased the property. The current operation is run by fourth-generation farmer Jamie Ager and his wife Amy. They focus on 100 percent grass-fed beef and pasture-raised pork, working with a network of partner farms across the Southeast to supply regional restaurants and grocery stores including Whole Foods and Ingles. You will find Hickory Nut Gap beef on menus all over Asheville, usually with the farm's name prominently listed.

This is your first warning: once you start reading menu sourcing notes, you will not be able to stop. Discomfort at uninformative menus follows quickly. It will happen faster than you expect.

Sunburst Trout Farms has been producing rainbow trout since 1948, when Dick Jennings started the first commercial trout farm east of the Mississippi — initially in Cashiers, later moving to Haywood County. The trout grow in water drawn from Lake Logan, a privately held lake in the Pisgah National Forest with no industry or agriculture upstream. The farm is now run by Jennings's grandsons, Wes and Ben Eason. Fish swimming in the morning can be on a restaurant plate the same evening.

After you have eaten trout that fresh, frozen trout will seem like a different species entirely.

Looking Glass Creamery was started in 2009 by Jennifer and Andy Perkins on a farm in Columbus, North Carolina. They milk 25 cows whose output goes directly into cheese aged in underground cellars on the same property. Their Drovers Road cheddar won a bronze medal at the World Championship Cheese Competition in 2024, scoring 98.275 out of 100 possible points in a field of more than 3,300 entries from 25 countries. Their cheese is available at Hickory Nut Gap Farm Store, South Slope Cheese Company, and on restaurant menus throughout the area.

This is the point at which your grocery shopping begins to resemble a background check. You will know the farm name, the breed of cow, and the county where the milk was produced before you commit to a purchase. You will find this completely normal. Other people in your life will not.

These are not the only farms in the region. They are representative of what's here. The Appalachian Sustainable Agriculture Project, known as ASAP, has been building the infrastructure connecting local farms to local buyers since the early 2000s. They publish an annual Local Food Guide listing farms throughout Western North Carolina and run programs connecting those farms to restaurants, schools, hospitals, and institutions. When Meherwan Irani opened Chai Pani in 2009 and reached out to source local ingredients, ASAP gave him a list of 50 farms he could work with immediately.

The system was already in place. It still is. That infrastructure — the network of farms, the distribution relationships, the community organizations maintaining them — is part of what makes Asheville's food culture durable rather than fashionable. Trends come and go. The farms were here before the trend and will be here after it, which is why the restaurants built on top of them tend to last.

The Tailgate Markets and the Texture of Daily Life

The term tailgate market in Western North Carolina refers to something specific, and explaining it is the kind of thing that makes you sound like a person who has become very serious about produce. It is a farmers market that takes place in a parking lot or open space, vendors selling directly from their farms, setting up tables and tents and whatever else they have hauled in that morning. The name is older than the format. The format is better than the name suggests.

Asheville has more than 20 of these markets operating throughout the area. The North Asheville Tailgate Market runs year-round on Saturday mornings at the UNC Asheville campus. The Asheville City Market runs downtown. The River Arts District Farmers Market operates on Saturdays. The West Asheville Tailgate Market has its own following. There are markets in surrounding communities: Weaverville, Black Mountain, Candler, and others.

For most of the year, there is at least one market within a reasonable drive on any given weekend, and often more than one during peak season. You can buy directly from the farmer who grew your vegetables, the cheesemaker who made your cheese, the person who smoked your trout. You can ask where the pig was raised, what the cows ate, how old the eggs are. You will ask. You will ask these questions without embarrassment, which is itself a sign that something has already gone wrong.

This proximity has a specific and irreversible practical effect. It will radicalize you. One heirloom tomato from a tailgate market in August, still warm from the vine, and you are permanently done with the pale, traveling spheres that pass for tomatoes in grocery stores every January. You will know this has happened when you find yourself in a supermarket produce aisle in February, picking up a tomato, putting it back down, and sighing in a way that will alarm other shoppers.

After fifteen minutes on a Saturday morning talking to the farmer who grew your salad greens, the grocery store version of that transaction will feel like a different activity entirely. You will know where your food came from. You will be able to picture the field. You will also be unable to stop talking about it.

This will strain at least one relationship.

Katie Button described standing at the North Asheville Tailgate Market before she opened Cúrate, floored by the quality and variety on offer: fairytale eggplants, beautiful peppers, vendors who could tell you the name of the field. That visit helped convince her to open in Asheville rather than somewhere else. The tailgate market did not just supply the restaurant. It recruited the chef.

This keeps happening. The market pulls in the chef. The chef opens the restaurant. The restaurant raises the standard. The standard raises the expectation. You arrive thinking you are looking for a nice place to live, and six months later you are on a first-name basis with a mushroom forager. This is the mechanism. Now you know how it works.

The Foodtopia Branding and Why It Works

In the early 2000s, Asheville's tourism office invented the word Foodtopia to describe the local culinary scene. Branded marketing language like this usually has a short shelf life: a moment of novelty followed by the slow embarrassment of repetition. Foodtopia somehow stuck.

Unlike most marketing coinages, it turned out to be accurate.

Travel and Leisure named Asheville the top foodie destination in the United States. Yelp named it the best city for foodie visitors in 2022. The New York Times — not given to hyperbole about mid-sized Southern cities — listed Chai Pani among America's favorite restaurants. The Washington Post's analysis of chain versus independent restaurant density identified Asheville as an outlier in the best possible way.

Asheville was also the first U.S. city designated as a Green Dining Destination by the Green Restaurant Association, which recognized its concentration of restaurants operating with sustainable practices. That designation predates many of the individual awards. It reflects something structural about how the food culture here operates — not just at the top of the market, but throughout it. The sustainable practices are not a branding exercise. They are the operating model, built into the sourcing, the staffing, the menus, and the relationships with farms that have been accumulating for decades. A designation like that is easy to give to a city with one or two high-profile sustainable restaurants. Giving it to Asheville meant recognizing that the practice had become the norm.

The Chow Chow Culinary Festival ran from 2019 through 2023 as Asheville's signature food event, drawing chefs, farmers, and food producers from across the region. It felt less like a festival and more like a community gathering with excellent cooking. Katie Button and Meherwan Irani were among its founders. Featured guests included James Beard-winning Appalachian food writer Ronni Lundy and Nobel Peace Prize nominee José Andrés.

In February 2024, the nonprofit behind it shut down permanently. Ticket sales never recovered to pre-pandemic levels. Financial losses mounted. In the end, 45 vendors from the 2023 festival were left unpaid, owed over $20,000 in promised honoraria the organization said it could not cover. It was a poor ending to something that had been genuinely well-regarded.

The impulse behind it was sound. The community it served is still here. This is not a city that runs low on things worth celebrating, which is part of the problem we have been describing this entire chapter.

Not every influential voice in Asheville's food scene has a culinary degree or a restaurant of their own. Stu Helm started writing about food to amuse his friends on Facebook and ended up spending twelve years doing it almost daily — a blog, a podcast, a radio show, a regular column on local sites including AshVegas.com, and an annual Best of Asheville Food Fan Awards that restaurants actually campaign for. He calls himself a food fan rather than a critic, and the distinction is genuine: his enthusiasms run from hot dogs to foraged mushrooms, and he covers both with the same attention. When Edible Asheville profiled him in 2019, they called him an influential voice in Asheville's restaurant scene, which is accurate but undersells it.

The influence is structural. Helm has guided Asheville Food Tours for nearly a decade, which means he has personally walked thousands of visitors through the neighborhoods and made the case, in real time on the sidewalk, for why the food here is different from anywhere else. He tracks every restaurant opening, follows the movement of local chefs from kitchen to kitchen, and maintains a running public record of what is worth eating and where. In a city with over 250 independent restaurants and no reliable chain fallback, that kind of ongoing civic documentation has real value. The chefs know him. The owners know him. He is the connective tissue between the kitchen and the customer, and he has been paying attention and writing it down since before anyone else thought it mattered.

What Hurricane Helene Actually Did

Any account of Asheville's food scene written in 2025 or 2026 has to address Hurricane Helene, which made landfall in late September 2024 and caused catastrophic flooding throughout Western North Carolina. The French Broad and Swannanoa rivers broke their banks at historic levels. Parts of the city and surrounding region were devastated. The damage to infrastructure, homes, businesses, and farms was severe and in some cases permanent.

Restaurants were among the hardest hit in a city where hospitality is one of the primary economic engines. Many closed immediately after the storm — some temporarily, some for good. The recovery was slow, uneven, and complicated by the scale of the disaster.

By the one-year mark in September 2025, a significant portion of Asheville's core restaurant community had survived, rebuilt, or reimagined itself. Chai Pani reopened. Cúrate reopened. The Market Place kept operating through it. Neng Jr's came back. Good Hot Fish returned. The breweries recovered. Some places did not make it back, and their absence matters.

The story is not finished for everyone.

And then, fourteen months after the floods, Michelin showed up with 15 recognitions. James Beard nominations followed in early 2026. A food scene that took decades to build, that survived a catastrophe that would have finished lesser cities, came back and somehow got more recognized on the other side of it. If you were hoping the disaster had made Asheville slightly less appealing, slightly easier to resist, that hope did not pan out.

A city that responds to its worst year by earning its first Michelin stars is not going to make your decision easy.

William Dissen does not talk about resilience in abstract terms. He talks about the farmers he still calls. The specific variety of apple he is waiting for. The trout season. The cheese. A food culture built on actual relationships with actual producers turns out to be harder to uproot than one built on supply chains and distributor catalogs. When the floods came, the restaurants that knew their farmers called them.

The farmers called back. The work continued.

The Mechanics of Actually Eating Here

You may be wondering what this means for a regular Tuesday. The answer is that Asheville is an unusually pleasant place to eat on a regular Tuesday, because the options scale from the nationally recognized down to the genuinely excellent neighborhood spot without much drop-off in quality.

The South Slope, a roughly mile-long stretch running south from downtown, contains nine breweries plus a dense concentration of restaurants. Chai Pani is here. So is Little

Chango, with its Puerto Rican arepas and Bib Gourmand recognition. Good Hot Fish, Bear's Smokehouse, Mother. The cuisines range from Indian street food to Caribbean to Southern fish camp, all within a few walkable blocks. Most nights you can decide where you're going after you've already left the house. This sounds like a small thing. It is not a small thing.

West Asheville, across the French Broad River from downtown, has its own strong restaurant identity: more neighborhood-oriented, less tourist-facing. Neng Jr's, The Admiral, and Sunny Point Cafe anchor a stretch of Haywood Road that rewards walking slowly and reading menus in windows. Weekend brunch lines here are their own social institution.

Biltmore Village sits just south of downtown, near the entrance to the Biltmore Estate. It has its own cluster of restaurants in a historic district of small stone buildings that is physically charming in the way that makes people pull out their phones to take pictures. Corner Kitchen, a farm-to-table bistro in a Tudor cottage that has been a neighborhood anchor since 2004, was badly flooded by Hurricane Helene and only recently finished a full rebuild and reopened. Locals were relieved. The food there ranges from casual to formal, and the whole neighborhood rewards a slow Saturday afternoon. Gemelli, the Italian-American restaurant from chef Anthony Cerrato that previously operated in the Westgate Shopping Center, opened its new location at 28 Hendersonville Road in April 2026, taking over a building that took nearly eleven feet of floodwater during Helene and has since been fully rebuilt.

The quality does not stop at the neighborhoods that get the most attention. In north Asheville, along Merrimon Avenue, Plant is a vegan fine-dining restaurant opened in 2011 by chef Jason Sellers that Food & Wine, USA Today, and PETA have all independently named among the best of its kind in the country. Non-vegans go regularly. Also on Merrimon is Vinnie's Neighborhood Italian, which has been voted Best Italian Restaurant in Asheville for over a decade by Mountain Xpress readers and holds a Hall of Fame distinction for Best Pasta. Owner Eric Scheffer, originally from Long Island, built the place around old-school New York Italian recipes passed down through family and friends, and it shows.

South Asheville has its own version of the same story. Vinnie's has a second location on Hendersonville Road, ranked in the Top 25 restaurants in the United States by TripAdvisor. Stone Bowl Korean, also on Hendersonville Road, is a neighborhood fixture where the signature dolsot bibimbap arrives sizzling in a heated stone bowl and the banchan keeps coming. It is the kind of place that makes the point without needing to: excellent, specific, international cooking is not a downtown-only phenomenon in Asheville.

In east Asheville, Copper Crown on Tunnel Road has been a quietly beloved neighborhood bistro since 2015, drawing on New American cooking with New Orleans and Southern influences, sourcing from local farms including Hickory Nut Gap, and filling up nightly with people who drove past a dozen chain restaurants to get there.

And then there is Le Parisien, which opened in February 2026 at 62 North Lexington Avenue downtown, in the very building where Bouchon used to be. Chef Gabriel Attala's classical French menu — tartiflette, steak au poivre, chocolate mousse — represents the kind of restaurant that shows up in Asheville regularly: serious cooking, a specific culinary identity, a chef who chose this city over other options. The point is not that any individual restaurant is remarkable. The point is that this keeps happening. Restaurants open. The standard does not drop. The list gets longer.

Downtown Asheville has wall-to-wall options in every direction from Pack Square — Chai Pani, Cúrate, The Market Place on Wall Street, and dozens of others at varying styles and price points. On weekend evenings in season, the lines outside the most popular places are real. Plan ahead or eat early.

The breweries function the way gastropubs function in other cities: you go for a drink and stay for the food and the company. Most have outdoor seating that fills in good weather. Most take the food seriously. The combination of excellent local beer and genuinely good food, in an outdoor setting with mountains nearby, is not something most cities offer at this casual a level.

What the full picture adds up to is a city where eating well does not require effort, planning, or money beyond what you would spend on food anywhere else. The price point at Asheville's best restaurants is not, in most cases, dramatically higher than comparable food in larger cities. The difference is that in Asheville, that price point delivers ingredients with a specific story, cooked by people who chose to be here rather than somewhere else. That specificity is what the James Beard Foundation recognized. It is what Michelin recognized. It is what people who move here recognize, usually around month three, usually at a Tuesday night dinner they almost did not bother to book.

The thing about all of this, taken together, is that it becomes your normal. Six months after moving here, you will stop registering it as remarkable that there are four different excellent options within walking distance on a Tuesday night. You will stop noticing how good the bread is at the cafe where you get coffee. You will take for granted that the restaurant you go to for a low-key birthday dinner can tell you exactly where the pork came from and what the pig ate. This is the real danger. Not that you will eat well in

Asheville. It's that eating well in Asheville will become your baseline, and then everything else will seem insufficient by comparison.

You have been warned.

The Uncomfortable Conclusion

Here is the problem with Asheville's food scene, stated plainly: it will recalibrate your expectations in ways you cannot fully anticipate before you experience it.

It is not that you will become a food snob, exactly. It is more that you will become aware of what food can be when it comes from a specific place and is handled by people who care about that place. The connection between the farm and the plate, which in most cities is invisible, becomes visible here.

And once you can see it, you cannot unsee it.

The recalibration happens slowly and then all at once. First you start noticing when restaurants list their farm sources. Then you start noticing when they don't. Then you start cooking differently at home, because you have been buying from tailgate markets and you know what ingredients can taste like at their best. Then you find yourself standing in a perfectly good grocery store in another city, holding a piece of cheese, and feeling a specific kind of low-grade sadness that you cannot fully explain to anyone who has not lived in Asheville.

You will start asking questions at restaurants that people in other cities do not ask. Where is this fish from? What farm is this pork from? Is this bread made from local grain? You will not ask these questions because you are difficult. You will ask them because Asheville has trained you to expect answers.

You will visit friends in other cities and feel vaguely sad at dinner, not because the food is bad, but because it does not have a story. You will stop at a chain restaurant on a road trip and feel briefly dislocated, the way you feel when you come home from somewhere interesting and your regular life seems slightly flat by comparison.

Your visiting relatives will spend the entire trip eating well. On the drive home, they will text you questions about how to find a tailgate market near them, whether the beer is actually that good, and whether you know how to make chaat.

You will tell them yes, you know a place. You will already be planning when to go back.

This is, obviously, a terrible outcome for anyone who had a perfectly comfortable relationship with food before moving here. We strongly advise against it.

CHAPTER TWO

DON'T MOVE HERE
IF YOU NEED TO GET AROUND

Let's get the bad news out of the way. Asheville does not have a real international airport. It doesn't have a real highway system, by any big-city standard. And its public transit, bless its heart, is doing what it can with what it has.

What Asheville does have is a road network designed for a much smaller city, a traffic situation that rewards creative profanity, and a $1.8 billion highway project that has been in planning since 1989 and is now, finally, under construction. The orange barrels are out. The cranes are coming. The city that spent thirty-seven years talking about this is now living with the consequences of actually doing it.

On the bright side: the airport is quite good. Let's start there.

The Problem With Small Airports (They're Too Easy)

The standard complaint about Asheville Regional Airport is delivered with great confidence by people who have never had to drive to Charlotte-Douglas or fight their way through Atlanta Hartsfield-Jackson. The complaint is this: not enough nonstop flights. And yes, that's technically true.

AVL does not fly nonstop to Bangkok. Or Tokyo. Or, on most days, Seattle. What it does offer, as of early 2026, is nonstop service to 26 destinations via five airlines: American, Delta, United, Allegiant, and Sun Country. That covers Atlanta, Charlotte, New York, Newark, Chicago, Washington D.C., Dallas-Fort Worth, Philadelphia, Las Vegas, Boston, Orlando, and Fort Lauderdale, plus a seasonal spread of Sun Belt destinations that grows the list considerably every winter.

Delta runs five to eight daily flights to Atlanta alone. American runs six to seven daily to Charlotte. Both cities are major hub airports, which means that once you land there, you can connect to essentially anywhere on earth. The indirect routing adds maybe ninety minutes to your journey. In exchange, you skip driving two hours just to reach the check-in counter.

That trade sounds worse than it is. Make it three times and it stops sounding like anything at all.

What "Regional" Actually Means Here

There is a particular kind of stress that belongs only to large airports. It begins in the parking structure. It builds through the check-in line, the bag drop, the TSA queue, the tram to the terminal, and the long walk to a gate that is somehow always at the absolute farthest point from where you started.

At AVL, you park your car, walk three minutes, check in, and go through security. On a normal day, car to gate runs under thirty minutes. On a good day, fifteen.

Locals describe this with a kind of dazed gratitude, the way people talk when they've been rescued from something they didn't fully realize was wrong until they were out of it. The first time you fly through a major hub and then come home through AVL, the contrast is almost disorienting. You walk off the plane, collect your bag, and you're outside in mountain air before your old airport would have finished boarding.

This is the problem with AVL. It removes a category of misery so completely that you stop noticing it, and then you can't imagine living without it. That is how Asheville works on people, generally. One thing at a time, until the prospect of leaving becomes difficult to explain.

A Brief Tour of What You're Avoiding

To fully appreciate AVL, it helps to spend a moment with the alternatives.

Charlotte-Douglas handles nearly 59 million passengers a year and is among the busiest airports in the United States. It is efficiently run. It is also an experience that begins the moment you turn off the interstate and enter the parking structure, which involves a shuttle, a line, and a quiet internal negotiation about whether you should have left earlier.

Once inside, Charlotte-Douglas has concourses labeled A through F. Concourse E and Concourse F are not adjacent. Getting between them is a project. If your connection is tight, it becomes an aerobic project.

Atlanta Hartsfield-Jackson is the busiest airport in the world by passenger volume. The main terminal connects to five concourses via an underground train called the Plane Train, which runs efficiently and is nonetheless a thing you must take just to reach your gate. The walk from your car to your aircraft seat is measured not in minutes but in fractions of a mile. On a bad day with a tight connection, the Plane Train becomes the central plot point of a story you will tell for years.

There is nothing wrong with either of these airports. They move enormous numbers of people every day with impressive competence. "Impressive competence at scale" is just not the same thing as "pleasant," and the difference is felt in the body rather than understood in the abstract.

AVL has one concourse. You walk to your gate. That's the whole system. It works.

Some people argue that the brisk efficiency of a small airport makes you soft, that the traveler who never navigates a six-gate connection at Hartsfield loses the alertness that major-airport transit demands. There may be something to this. What AVL will do is get you home without a story about it, which turns out to be what most people actually want from an airport.

The Hour Before Your Flight

At a major hub, the hour before departure belongs to the airport. It goes toward parking logistics, security at industrial scale, the long walk, finding a seat at a gate that has somehow filled before your flight was called. The airport owns that hour and charges you for the privilege.

At AVL, that hour is yours. Leave your house when a normal person would leave, drive twelve minutes south to Fletcher, park without strategy, clear security, and still have time for coffee before boarding. This is how Asheville captures people. Not with drama or spectacle, but with the quiet removal of friction, one small inconvenience at a time, until the city has quietly colonized your expectations and you can't remember what you were supposed to be complaining about.

Fletcher itself is not the point. It is a stretch of US-25 populated by car dealerships, storage facilities, and chain restaurants that exist because someone has to feed people near airports. Your first view arriving from elsewhere will be underwhelming. The mountains visible on the drive north twelve minutes later are doing all the work Fletcher cannot.

The Geography Lesson Nobody Asked For

Asheville sits at roughly 2,134 feet above sea level in the southern Appalachians. Getting here by car from any direction involves mountains. This is not news to anyone who has consulted a map.

What's sometimes undersold is how this geography actually simplifies the airport question. Charlotte is about two hours east on I-26 and I-85. Atlanta is three and a half hours south. Knoxville is roughly an hour and forty-five minutes northwest on I-40 through the Smoky Mountains.

All three cities have major international airports. For anyone with truly global travel requirements, connecting through one of them is perfectly viable. But the math only works if you live close enough to make the drive sensible, and Asheville residents emphatically do not. Most trips, most of the time, the calculation comes out in favor of flying out of AVL and connecting through Atlanta or Charlotte.

There is also the matter of what those drive times actually feel like. Anyone who has spent a Tuesday morning on I-285 around Atlanta, or watched the GPS quietly recalculate around an accident on I-77 into Charlotte, has a visceral understanding of why "just drive to the hub" is sometimes more aspiration than plan.

The Road In Is the Road Out

One thing worth saying about Asheville's geography: it connects to everything you actually want to reach when driving makes sense.

The Great Smoky Mountains National Park is about an hour west. Brevard and the Pisgah National Forest, home to hundreds of miles of trails and the famous Sliding Rock natural waterslide, are about thirty minutes south. The Blue Ridge Parkway essentially begins at Asheville's back door, and it is consistently rated among the most beautiful drives in America. Hendersonville is thirty minutes south. Black Mountain, a small community with its own arts scene, is twenty minutes east.

For someone who values outdoor access alongside urban life, this geography is the whole argument. The mountains are not just scenery. They are destinations. They are close. Getting to them, however, requires roads through mountains, and that is where the conversation gets complicated.

The I-40 Situation, Which Deserves Its Own Section

Interstate 40 through the Pigeon River Gorge is the main westbound route out of Asheville, connecting the city to Knoxville and points beyond. On a clear October day, with the hardwoods turning orange and gold on the slopes above and the Pigeon River running cold and white alongside, it is one of the more spectacular stretches of interstate in the eastern United States. Rock walls rise directly from the shoulder on one side. The river runs fast and emphatic on the other, deeply unconcerned about anyone's travel schedule.

"On a clear day" is doing a lot of work in that sentence.

The gorge has a long and distinguished history of complicating plans. The road was cut into a slope that the Pigeon River has been methodically undermining for millennia, and the river has not modified its behavior on account of the pavement. Rockslides are a recurring fact of life here, not dramatic enough to make national news but frequent enough that locals develop an instinct for checking conditions before committing to the westbound on-ramp on a rainy April morning.

Fog is the other variable. The gorge funnels weather the way it funnels the river, with focus and intensity. Fog that develops on humid mornings can reduce visibility from "scenic" to "inadvisable" in the span of a quarter mile. It sits in pockets. You drive into a clear stretch, relax, and then find a dense white wall with your headlights doing essentially decorative work.

Locals learn the fog zones the way sailors learn their harbors: specifically, experientially, and with respect.

Then there is the truck traffic. I-40 through the gorge is a primary freight corridor, and the trucks that use it are not the kind that hurry. A fully loaded eighteen-wheeler descending from the Tennessee side is a physics demonstration in slow motion: the driver rides the brakes, the engine brakes engage with a sound that echoes off the rock walls, and the line of cars behind develops a collective patience that is either calming or maddening depending on how late you are. Passing opportunities are limited. The gorge does not offer many straight sections.

None of this makes I-40 a bad road. It makes it a mountain road, which is a specific category with specific expectations. You leave a few minutes early. You check the weather. You know about the alternate, I-26 north through Kingsport to I-81 south, not because you expect to need it, but because mountain people keep alternates in their back pocket the way flat-state people keep an umbrella.

Most of the time the gorge is fine. The river is beautiful. The drive is one of the better ones in the region. The only inconvenience is the semi doing forty on the downgrade while you count the passing zones.

Asheville has highway access in four directions. The gorge is the western one, and it is worth knowing. It is not, by any reasonable measure, worth being afraid of.

The Airport That Couldn't Take a Hint

Here is where the story takes an inconvenient turn for anyone hoping the airport situation would discourage relocation.

In 2025, the year the airport chose to demolish its old terminal and begin a $400 million construction project, Asheville Regional Airport welcomed 2.24 million passengers. The second-busiest year in its history. Despite the construction inconvenience, despite the outdoor boarding, despite everything a mountain airport's logistics can present, the people kept coming.

The airport authority announced this with what can only be described as unseemly enthusiasm. The CEO declared it a reflection of the region's "continued appeal." One imagines a longtime Asheville resident putting down the newspaper with the quiet resignation of someone watching their favorite hiking trail get a parking fee and a visitor center.

The construction is called AVL Forward, and it is the largest capital investment in the airport's history. Four hundred million dollars. A new terminal. Two concourses. Twelve gates. Jet bridges at every single one of them. The new ticket lobby opened in June 2025. A new North Concourse followed two weeks later. The old terminal came down in October 2025. The full project runs about four and a half years from groundbreaking.

The outdoor boarding during construction remains the most defensible complaint about AVL. It is also temporary. The airport is being systematically improved into something very difficult to complain about, which is, if you already live here, a deeply annoying development.

The Living Wall Problem

The designers of the AVL Forward expansion have made some choices that reveal a great deal about what this city thinks of itself.

The new terminal will have river-inspired flooring patterns. Waterfall-influenced ceilings. A living wall in the baggage claim area, actual plants, requiring actual maintenance, installed in the room where you wait for your suitcase to appear.

This is not the design vocabulary of a facility trying to move people through efficiently and send them on their way. This is the design vocabulary of an airport that wants you to feel the Blue Ridge before you've even collected your bags. It is, depending on your perspective, either a lovely civic gesture or a highly effective advertisement for the mountains you're about to enter. Either way, it is exactly the kind of detail that makes people standing at a baggage carousel think they should probably come back.

The Art Deco buildings downtown survived because there was no money to demolish them. The airport is being built with living walls because there is now money to do things properly, and Asheville's definition of "properly" has always included the conviction that beauty is not an extravagance. That continuity of sensibility, from the S&W Building's terra cotta facade to the waterfall ceilings of a baggage claim, is either inspiring or maddening. The response probably tells you something about whether you'd be happy here.

Parking, Which Is Also Part of the Story

Parking at a major airport is expensive, far away, or both, managed by a company treating the experience as a revenue stream with no visible ceiling.

AVL does not operate this way. The airport offers multiple options within walking distance of the terminal at pricing that is, by any comparable standard, quite reasonable.

This sounds minor. Over years of regular travel, it is not

minor. It accumulates into yet another thing you will quietly stop wanting to give up, which is precisely the trap. Asheville is full of traps like this. They arrive disguised as conveniences.

A Brief Detour Into Why Asheville Has Anything at All

Understanding why Asheville has a good airport, a distinctive downtown, and more Art Deco architecture than any American city outside of Miami requires a short stop in some unusual economic history.

In the early twentieth century, Asheville was booming. The railroad arrived in 1880, when the city's population was about 2,000, and within two decades tourism money was pouring in. The 1920s brought a construction frenzy backed by civic optimism and, as it turned out, the highest per-capita municipal debt burden in the United States. When the Depression arrived, other cities defaulted or restructured. Asheville decided to pay every cent back. That took until 1976.

This decision had consequences nobody anticipated. Because Asheville spent four decades paying off Depression-era debt, it couldn't afford to demolish its older buildings and replace them with whatever was fashionable in the 1950s and 1960s. The Art Deco city hall finished in 1928, the S&W Cafeteria Building with its cream and turquoise terra cotta facade, the Jackson Building, the first skyscraper in the western Carolinas, all of it survived because there was no money for demolition. What felt like civic failure turned out, fifty years later, to be the thing that made downtown Asheville unlike any other downtown in the state.

Charlotte did the sensible thing: borrow, restructure, demolish, rebuild. Its skyline rivals any city in the South. It has almost no 1920s commercial architecture. Asheville, frozen by debt into involuntary preservation, kept its twenties.

The constraint became the character. The character became the draw. The draw became the traffic problem on Merrimon Avenue. These things are connected.

Here is what the Art Deco buildings are actually telling you, if you care to listen. They are not a preservation victory. They are evidence of a city that chose the hardest possible path, held to it for fifty years when every reasonable person would have found an easier way out, and emerged regarding its own stubbornness as a virtue. The buildings that survived are a monument to a place that will not be talked out of a position it has decided to hold. That is charming when it results in a beautiful downtown. It is less charming when the position being held is, say, a zoning dispute, or a road design, or an argument about a flyover versus an underpass that has now outlasted most of the people who started it.

This pattern, doing things that look impractical from the outside and treating the difficulty as confirmation of their rightness, runs through Asheville's approach to everything, including infrastructure. The preference for permanence over the quick fix is almost pathological. If you move here, you are moving among people who are hardwired this way. They will be your neighbors, your city council members, your fellow citizens in every future argument about how this place should be. You have been warned. The buildings are the warning.

The Honest Caveat

None of this is to suggest that AVL is perfect or that it offers everything a major metro airport does. It does not.

West Coast flights involve a connection. International travel is always at least one stop away. On routes that run once or twice daily, a mechanical delay or weather cancellation can mean a meaningful disruption. These are real limitations. They are also, for most people's actual travel patterns, less significant than they sound in the abstract.

The average American takes roughly two to four domestic trips per year. Even for frequent travelers, nonstop long-haul international routes are a small fraction of total journeys. The daily reality of airport access is dominated by short domestic trips, business travel to major cities, and vacation flights to places AVL covers well.

What AVL doesn't cover well is the edge case: the traveler flying internationally every month, or the person who needs to reach somewhere obscure on twelve hours' notice. If that describes you, living two hours from Charlotte or three and a half from Atlanta is a real constraint worth factoring in. For most people considering Asheville, the airport resolves itself within a few months into something between "fine" and "actually pretty good." Which is not a ringing endorsement. It's an honest one.

The Commute That Isn't

Asheville's average commute runs roughly 18 minutes each way, based on Census data. That puts it well below the national average of 27.6 minutes and dramatically below what accumulates in major metro areas. New York averages 37 minutes. Washington D.C. comes in at 34.8. San Francisco at 34.1.

Before you start calculating how many hours a year you'll reclaim, consider what the average is actually hiding. Asheville's terrain does not distribute commute times evenly. The mountains that make the city beautiful have also arranged the road network into a set of bottlenecks that the average cannot explain and that no GPS can route around, because there is no route around them. There is only through.

The city is organized around several distinct neighborhoods connected by a limited number of river crossings and ridge roads. Between West Asheville and downtown, two bridges carry the bulk of the traffic: the Amboy Road bridge and the Patton Avenue bridge. On a normal weekday morning, both of them are doing work that four bridges would struggle with. The consequence is simple and brutal. Miss the 7:45 departure window by twenty minutes and you will sit. You will watch the clock. You will consider, not for the first time, whether the people who designed this road network had ever actually tried to use it. No alternate routes will present themselves. The hills have seen to that. You are in the funnel, and the funnel has one exit, and it is also the funnel.

This is not a temporary condition. It is not something the I-26 Connector will fully fix, at least not for years. It is the price of living in a city built across ridges and river valleys, where the scenery and the traffic are products of exactly the same geography, and neither is going anywhere.

The average is real. The outliers are also real. The commute from West Asheville across the French Broad and up into North Asheville at 8:30 on a school-day morning is not an 18-minute experience. This is not a reversible condition.

The Airlines Keep Coming Anyway

Five airlines. Twenty-six nonstop destinations. Multiple daily flights to two of the world's busiest hub airports. This is what AVL offers as of early 2026, and the route map keeps expanding in ways that make the airport increasingly difficult to use as a reason not to move here.

Delta runs five to eight daily flights to Atlanta alone. American runs six to seven daily to Charlotte. United covers Newark and Chicago. Allegiant runs Florida routes that fill reliably. Sun Country rounds out the mix with seasonal leisure destinations. Austin, Denver, Minneapolis, Houston, and Miami have all appeared on the schedule at various points, which means the effective destination count is larger than any single month suggests. Airlines do not fly seasonal routes to places where people aren't going.

Growing airports attract more routes. More routes make the airport more useful. A more useful airport is harder to leave. The new twelve-gate terminal with its jet bridges and its living wall in baggage claim is not being built for the Asheville that existed ten years ago. It is being built for the Asheville that is arriving, faster than anyone who already lives here would prefer.

What You Actually Hear From People Who Live Here

Residents who moved to Asheville from larger cities talk about the airport in a consistent way. The concern before the move was limited nonstop options. The experience after the move is almost always that the concern was overblown.

Some people discover they travel less than they thought they did. Some find the network covers their destinations well enough. Some decide the extra Atlanta connection is a minor inconvenience in a daily life that is otherwise considerably better than the one they left. A few find it genuinely limiting, usually international business travelers or people with family in places requiring multiple connections.

For most people considering Asheville, the airport stops being a topic of conversation within the first year. Not because it's perfect. Because it's fine, and fine turns out to be enough when everything else is working.

One More Thing About the History

The first train to reach Asheville pulled in on October 3, 1880. Before that, the city was genuinely isolated in a way that's hard to fully imagine. The mountains that make the drive scenic also made the region nearly inaccessible for most of its early history.

The first real attempt at a road came with the Buncombe Turnpike, built between 1824 and 1828. It ran seventy-five miles from the South Carolina border to the Tennessee border along the French Broad River, and was considered the finest road in North Carolina, a lower bar than it sounds, given that competing routes involved conditions one traveler described as "gullies, and rocks, and rivers."

The turnpike's primary function was moving livestock. Drovers pushed enormous herds south from Tennessee and Kentucky toward markets in Charleston and Augusta. At peak season, an estimated 150,000 to 175,000 hogs passed through Asheville in a single fall. Not a year. A fall.

The noise was constant, grunt and squeal, bellow of cattle, clop of horses and mules on gravel. The mud was spectacular, as tens of thousands of hooves worked the road into something resembling the floor of a very large and poorly maintained barn. Zebulon Vance, then a young lawyer who would later serve as governor, described the town during drive season: "The rain continues to fall, and our streets are almost impassible with the mud and thousands upon thousands of hogs moving through the town adds to the general filthyness of everything around." He was not exaggerating for effect.

The smell was its own phenomenon. Inns sprang up every mile along the route to shelter man and animal alike, and corn became the region's first cash crop, planted specifically to feed the procession. The whole apparatus, the road, the inns, the corn, the mud, the smell, was the engine that made Asheville viable before tourism, before the railroad, before anything else. It was not a comfortable system. It was an effective one, which in Asheville's history has always been considered close enough.

The railroad changed everything, and quickly. When the Western North Carolina Railroad finally threaded its way through the mountains after years of engineering struggles and at least one stretch of track laid on grades that made experienced railroaders nervous, the city's population was about 2,000. Within twenty years it had multiplied several times over. Hotels went up. Tourists arrived by the trainload, seeking clean mountain air and the appeal of a city tucked into the ridgelines. The debt that followed was spectacular in its ambition. Both the ambition and the consequences are still visible, if you know where to look.

Two centuries after the hogs and fifty years after the railroad boom collapsed under Depression-era debt, 2.24 million passengers moved through Asheville Regional Airport in a single year. They collected their bags beneath a future living wall and dispersed into the mountains in rental cars. The smell situation was considerably improved. The fundamental dynamic had not changed much at all: Asheville as a place through which large numbers of people pass on their way to somewhere beautiful.

The hogs moved on. The people kept coming. The mountains, it turns out, are not a very effective deterrent.

The Daily Local Traffic, Which Is Its Own Story

Here is what the airport conversation misses, because the airport is twelve miles south of town and most of your flying happens a few times a year. Here is what you will encounter every single day.

Merrimon Avenue is the main artery running north from downtown through North Asheville, past the coffee shops and grocery stores and yoga studios and elementary schools. On a Tuesday morning at 8:15, it is a parking lot with delusions. Two lanes in most sections, one each way, serving a corridor that has grown considerably in population and commercial density since anyone thought carefully about whether two lanes would be sufficient. The answer, arrived at empirically each morning, is that they are not.

Hendersonville Road runs south from downtown toward Biltmore Village and the airport, and it presents the same situation from a different compass point. Busy in ways that punish the optimist. If you live south of downtown and work anywhere north of Biltmore, you will spend a measurable portion of your commute waiting at the light at Biltmore Avenue, reconsidering your life choices, watching the same three cars fail to merge from the turn lane before the signal changes again.

The city's geography compounds all of this. Asheville is not flat. It is built across ridges and river valleys, which is part of why it looks the way it does and part of why the road network requires so much creative routing. There are very few straight lines of any useful length. Major roads follow river valleys and ridgelines rather than a logical grid, which means the distance from point A to point B as the crow flies bears almost no relationship to the distance as the car drives.

You will eventually learn the shortcuts. The learning process takes longer than you expect and involves at least one wrong turn down a road that narrows to a single lane and ends at someone's barn.

None of this is catastrophic. But it is daily, and daily adds up.

The Bus, God Bless It

Asheville has a public transit system called ART, which stands for Asheville Redefines Transit. This is either an aspirational statement or an admission that the old definition needed work.

The system runs bus routes throughout the city and is

staffed by people doing their jobs conscientiously under significant constraints. Those constraints are real. Asheville's bus network uses a hub-and-spoke model centered downtown, which means getting from one part of the city to another often requires a trip through downtown regardless of whether downtown is remotely between where you are and where you're going. Frequency on most routes is thirty to sixty minutes. Service ends in the early evening on most lines.

There is no light rail. There is no commuter rail. There is no realistic prospect of either in the near term, because Asheville's terrain and relatively small population make fixed-rail transit extremely expensive to build and difficult to route. The city has generally resolved this in favor of acknowledging the car's dominance and investing in road improvements, a reasonable conclusion that is also deeply unsatisfying to anyone who sold their car before moving here.

What Buncombe County does have, quietly doing its job without much fanfare, is Mountain Mobility. It is not glamorous. It is, however, real.

Mountain Mobility is the county's community transportation system, established in 1989 to serve residents outside the city's ART network. It runs three Trailblazer routes, connecting Black Mountain, Enka-Candler, and the North Buncombe corridor through Weaverville and Woodfin to the ART system, so a resident without a car in Weaverville can, in theory, piece together a trip to downtown Asheville without owning a vehicle. The Trailblazer buses are fare-free, lift-equipped, and run Monday through Friday. The vehicles seat fourteen to eighteen passengers and have bike racks, because this is Asheville and of course they do.

For older and disabled residents, Mountain Mobility offers something more pointed. There is a free monthly ART bus pass for residents sixty-five and older. There is the RIDE voucher program, which lets eligible elderly and disabled residents purchase transportation at twenty-five percent of the standard rate. There is demand-response service, meaning someone schedules a ride and a van shows up. It is not the subway. It is a system designed around the specific reality of a mountain county where car ownership is assumed, frailty arrives eventually, and the gap between those two facts needs something to fill it.

The honest context: Mountain Mobility works best for people who can plan ahead and travel during off-peak hours between ten and two. It was not designed to replace daily commuting. It was designed to keep people connected when other options narrow, which in a region with Asheville's demographics is a more pressing problem than the transit conversation usually acknowledges.

If you are planning to live in Asheville without a car, it is possible in a limited way. The downtown core is walkable enough. Pack Square, the River Arts District, and the South Slope brewery district are all reachable on foot, though "reachable" on the South Slope means negotiating a steep, patchy network of industrial streets that were not designed with pedestrians in mind and have not since reconsidered. The South Slope occupies a former industrial corridor wedged between a ridge and the railroad, which gives it character and also gives it grades that will test anyone arriving on foot from downtown expecting a gentle stroll. Its charms are real. Its topography is also real. Plan accordingly.

Cycling is a similar story. The French Broad River Greenway offers a flat, scenic route connecting several neighborhoods without requiring anyone to battle traffic. For recreation and errands within a limited radius, a bike genuinely works. For getting across town on a Tuesday morning when you have somewhere to be by nine, the hills have opinions and they will share them.

The honest summary: Asheville is a car city. You will need one. You will occasionally sit on Merrimon Avenue and wonder if there was ever a plan. The answer is yes. It is called the I-26 Connector, and it has been forthcoming for thirty-seven years.

The I-26 Connector, Which Deserves Its Own Section (and Then Some)

The I-26 Connector is a $1.8 billion infrastructure project that will eventually connect Interstate 26 from the south side of Asheville to US 19-23-70 on the north side, running a new section of interstate through the city across the French Broad River and rerouting highway traffic away from downtown. The project has been in planning since 1989. Construction began in 2025. You do not need to know much more than that to understand the situation.

Here is what the next decade looks like from the inside. Orange barrels on the south sections already. The main north section is not far behind. Lane closures appearing without warning and vanishing without apology. Detours that add ten minutes to trips you have made a thousand times, across intersections that are now reconfigured in ways that are technically correct and feel completely wrong. Contractor equipment on streets that previously had other purposes. The low continuous rumble of machinery starting before dawn, because large infrastructure projects do not keep civilian hours and neither, it turns out, will you.

Every grocery run is a navigational problem now. Every school drop-off is a route that used to exist and no longer does. The mental map you built of this city, the one that told you which lane to be in three blocks before the turn, the one that knew which lights to avoid at which hours, all of it is being demolished and rebuilt in real time, slightly wrong for years, until the project finishes and you build a new one. This is the price of living in a city doing something it should have done in the 1990s. The inconvenience is real. It is also, technically, progress. Those two things are allowed to be true at the same time.

The design of the project has its own controversy, centered on a planned eight-lane elevated structure over Patton Avenue in West Asheville that was not in the original agreement and is still being contested. The community arguing against it has been arguing since before most of the people who recently moved here arrived. They will still be arguing when the orange barrels come down. This is Asheville. Stubbornness is not a bug. It is load-bearing.

Businesses have been displaced. A beloved music venue on Riverside Drive that had become one of the city's genuine gathering places is gone from its original site. Residential properties have been acquired. Each of these has its own story, and residents who have been here long enough know them. The city is being physically reorganized to accommodate a future that the people who planned it could not quite see, and the people living in it now are absorbing the cost.

When the project finishes, Asheville will have a highway system matched to the city it has become. The official completion date is 2031. Apply the standard adjustment. Plan accordingly.

The Train That May or May Not Come

I told you earlier we have no commuter rail. That is still true. But the state began teasing us with something else in earnest around 2023...

Passenger rail is the longest of the long games, and longer horizons are where Asheville's civic optimism historically gets tested most severely. The proposed $650 million rail line would run approximately 139 miles from Salisbury through Statesville and Hickory to Asheville, restoring service that ran until 1975 and has been conspicuously absent ever since. The state's own rail plan calls the corridor critical. The federal government has started funding the planning process. Neither of those things is a train. But both of them, fifteen years ago, would have seemed like a fantasy.

The case for it is not complicated: a region of this geography cannot build its way to transportation adequacy on roads alone. The mountains that constrain development also constrain highway capacity. There are only so many routes through the ridgelines, and the ones that exist are already at capacity during peak hours in ways that anyone trying to get somewhere at five o'clock on a Friday already understands. If you can live in Black Mountain or Weaverville or Marion and commute to Asheville by train, the drive-time math that currently limits where workers can realistically live starts to look different. That distinction changes residential location decisions in ways that road expansions generally don't, because you can do things on a train that you cannot do in a car on I-40.

Whether it actually gets built is a question with no clean answer. The planning process has more phases ahead of it than behind it, and Amtrak projects possible service could begin as early as 2034 if federal and state funding aligns. What's worth noting is that the conversation is happening at all. Asheville is being treated as a destination worth connecting to a passenger rail network rather than an afterthought. That is a shift. It reflects the same demographic and economic momentum driving everything else in this chapter, and it is a reasonably reliable signal of how seriously the region's growth is being taken by people who make decisions about where rail money goes.

The affordable housing bond, the GO bonds, the rail planning, the wage strategy: these are not the achievements of a city that decided to coast on its reputation. They're the achievements of a city arguing with itself about what growth requires and occasionally arriving at something that looks like a collective decision. That argument is ongoing and sometimes unpleasant. It's also the sign of a place that hasn't stopped caring, which counts for more than it might appear.

The Real Verdict on Getting In, Out, and Around

Asheville is not a city you move to because it has a world-class international hub airport, a seamless road network, or a robust public transit system. It has none of those things, and it is actively spending several billion dollars over the next decade trying to fix the second problem while doing very little structural about the third.

What it does have is an airport that works reasonably well for most people's actual travel needs and is getting bigger. A local traffic situation that is manageable once you stop expecting it to behave like somewhere else. A downtown core that is walkable, if you are already in it. A commute that is, on average and in good conditions, genuinely short.

These are not nothing. They are the accumulated texture of daily life, and they add up in ways that only become visible after you've lived here long enough to compare.

There is a version of Asheville's transportation situation that sounds like a liability. That version is correct, and anyone selling you aggressively on how fine everything is has probably forgotten what it's like to move somewhere new and discover the gaps. The gaps are real. So is everything else. Most people who move here decide the arithmetic works. A few decide it doesn't. Both groups are right about their own lives.

A Closing Thought on the Getting-Around Problem

People who haven't lived in Asheville worry about the airport before they move. People who've lived here a year don't think about it much at all. People who've lived here five years occasionally bring it up to new arrivals with a slightly wicked look, curious to see how long before the concern quietly dissolves.

It usually takes about three trips.

The first time you clear security in twelve minutes and realize your gate is forty feet away, something shifts. The second time you park for four days and pay less than a tank of gas, something settles. By the third trip, you've stopped comparing AVL to airports in cities you no longer live in.

The traffic on Merrimon Avenue you stop comparing to anywhere else after about a month. You just start leaving ten minutes earlier.

The mountains make up for a lot. This is not a reversible condition.

CHAPTER THREE

DON'T MOVE HERE
IF YOU CAN'T AFFORD IT

Asheville has a reputation problem, and the problem is that all the reputations are accurate simultaneously.

It is a small mountain city of roughly 95,000 people that appears reliably on national lists of the best places to live, the best food cities, the best outdoor destinations, and the most desirable mid-size cities in the American South. It has a Michelin-recognized dining scene, a music venue where nationally touring acts compete to play, and approximately one million acres of protected wilderness within a short drive in any direction. People who visit it tend to leave with an unsettling sense that they should probably be living here instead.

It also has home prices at roughly 6.5 times the area median income, the highest ratio in North Carolina. Average rents north of $1,700 a month. An average local salary that runs about 16 percent below the state average. And a renter wage gap that ranks seventh worst in the entire country.

These facts coexist without any apparent embarrassment. Asheville is genuinely wonderful and genuinely expensive, and it has been both things for long enough that residents have largely stopped finding the combination surprising. The people who move here and stay have generally worked out, in advance or shortly after arriving, how to make the math function. The people who don't work it out tend to leave. Both groups usually admit, unprompted, that they loved it while they were there.

This chapter is about the math.

What the Lists Measure and What They Don't

Every year, various publications compile rankings of the best places to live and work in America. Asheville appears on them reliably, often near the top of categories like best for quality of life, best mid-size city, and best for outdoor access. The pitch is always the same: vibrant arts scene, outdoor culture, great food, creative energy, friendly people, mountain air. All of it is accurate.

What the lists measure less precisely is what any of this costs, or what the local economy pays the people who live there. A city where you can eat extraordinarily well, hike a world-class trail, and catch a nationally touring band on a Tuesday night sounds like a bargain. Whether it actually is depends entirely on what you earn and what you pay to be there.

The gap between Asheville's desirability and its affordability is not new, and it is not accidental. It is the predictable result of a place that became very appealing very quickly, attracted significant outside investment and in-migration, and did not build housing fast enough to absorb any of it. A 2025 housing needs assessment commissioned by the Land of Sky Regional Council found that the Asheville region must add 34,358 dwelling units over the next five years just to meet current demand: 13,921 rental units and more than 20,400 for-sale homes. To put that in terms a local would understand, 34,358 is also roughly the number of Subaru Outbacks currently ahead of you in traffic on I-26 at any given moment on a Friday afternoon, so the scale of the problem should feel familiar.

Two-thirds of all neighborhoods in Asheville are currently zoned exclusively for single-family homes. That structure, largely unchanged for decades, is the physical reason the housing supply has not kept pace with demand. You cannot build enough homes for a growing city if the rules governing most of its land only permit one home per lot. Asheville is aware of this, and the policy debate about what to do is active, contentious, and proceeding at the speed of municipal politics, which is to say: slowly.

The broader regional context is worth noting. Buncombe County now has the highest median home list price of any county in North Carolina covering an urban core, higher even than Wake County, which contains Raleigh, and Mecklenburg County, which contains Charlotte. This is a city that, by the numbers, has priced itself above the two largest metro areas in a state that has been one of the fastest-growing in the country.

What Things Actually Cost

Housing is the number that shapes everything else. The market has shifted enough in the past year that the numbers are less alarming than they were at the peak, which is a little like saying your dental bill is less terrifying than your hospital bill. Both are still real.

The median home sale price in Asheville spent most of 2025 around $500,000, then softened to roughly $440,000 by year's end, with Buncombe County holding a bit steadier at $477,000. The more important number is what you'd need to earn to buy a median-priced home with a standard 20 percent down payment: $112,726 a year. In a city where the average salary runs closer to $48,900, that figure is less a qualification threshold than a polite suggestion addressed to someone who doesn't live here. To reach it through local employment alone, you'd need to hold roughly two and a half full-time jobs simultaneously, ideally without sleeping between shifts.

There is a category called workforce housing, defined as homes affordable to families earning up to 120 percent of area median income, with a ceiling around $372,400. The share of Asheville's for-sale housing gap made up of homes below that price is 68 percent. In other words, the homes most working people here could theoretically afford represent the largest piece of the shortage. Supply and demand are both present; they have simply agreed to ignore each other.

Homes below $400,000 in the Asheville area are genuinely scarce and tend to move quickly. The broader market has softened from its pandemic-era frenzy, and inventory has risen to around four to five months of supply as of early 2026, with homes sitting on the market for an average of about 66 days, compared to 47 days in 2024. That is welcome news for buyers who felt the ultra-competitive conditions of recent years. It is less transformative news for someone who needed the market to get meaningfully cheaper rather than just slightly less frantic.

Where you buy within the metro matters as much as whether you buy. Downtown Asheville and the immediately surrounding neighborhoods, Montford, the South Slope, West Asheville's walkable core along Haywood Road, command the highest prices, consistently running above the city median and often well above it. North Asheville, with its larger lots and proximity to the University of North Carolina Asheville, sits in the same premium tier.

South Asheville, built out more recently with larger homes and easy access to the Biltmore area, draws buyers who want more square footage and newer construction, and it prices accordingly. East Asheville and the areas along

Tunnel Road have historically offered slightly more accessible entry points, though that gap has been closing steadily. The neighborhoods that drew artists and young families a decade ago with their relative affordability are now the neighborhoods people mention when they talk about how much things have changed. This is the standard arc of a desirable city, and Asheville has been running it on schedule.

Asheville's price-to-income ratio sits at 6.5 times, the highest in North Carolina and comparable not to Raleigh or Charlotte but to Boston. The ratio was around 3x in the 1990s and 4.5x in the 2010s. The trend line is not subtle.

Boston, for those keeping track, has the Atlantic Ocean and a baseball team with actual rings. Asheville has different selling points. Evidently they are sufficient.

Renting is not a comfortable alternative to buying. Average rents in Asheville as of early 2026 run between $1,600 and $1,800 a month, with one-bedrooms around $1,500 to $1,600 and two-bedrooms in the $1,740 to $1,900 range. After rapid increases through mid-2025, rents have leveled off and in some categories edged down slightly, which counts as good news in a market that had been conducting itself like it had somewhere to be.

To afford a one-bedroom without spending more than 30 percent of your income on housing, you need to be earning just under $60,000 a year. About 45 percent of Asheville renters do not clear that bar, which means nearly half the city is spending so much on rent that supporting the local arts economy, buying a barista's EP, or attending a ceramicist's opening is a luxury decision rather than a casual Thursday. Nearly 20 percent are in worse shape than that, with rent consuming more than half their take-home.

Groceries, utilities, and transportation in Asheville run

modestly above national averages, but it is housing that dominates the budget math. A single person needs roughly $50,000 to $60,000 annually to cover rent and basic expenses with modest savings. Shared housing can bring that threshold down to around $40,000 to $45,000 per person. These numbers are not impossible, but they require either a local income that clears the bar or one that arrives from somewhere the bar is set higher.

What Things Pay

The average annual salary in Asheville is approximately $48,900, about 16 percent below the North Carolina state average and roughly 23 percent below the national average. The median household income sits at $71,102, a figure pulled upward significantly by remote workers earning salaries pegged to more expensive markets and by retirees drawing on accumulated wealth from careers spent elsewhere. Strip those populations out and the income picture for people dependent on local wages looks considerably thinner.

The gap between those numbers and what the city costs is not abstract. It shows up in the specific calculations people run when they are deciding whether to stay. A teacher at a Buncombe County school earns between $50,000 and $65,000 depending on experience, which is a real salary that goes a meaningful distance in most of North Carolina and not quite far enough here. A social worker, a librarian, a nonprofit program manager: these are the careers that communities depend on and that Asheville's job market reliably produces at wages that make the housing math genuinely uncomfortable. The people doing the work that keeps a city functional are, in many cases, the people for whom the city has become the least financially forgiving.

The local job market is dominated by healthcare, tourism, hospitality, and retail. Mission Hospital is the largest employer in the region, and beyond healthcare, the employment picture is built substantially around serving the visitors and residents who make Asheville attractive to begin with. Hotel managers earn $45,000 to $65,000. Restaurant managers earn $38,000 to $52,000. These are supervisory roles with real career trajectories, and they represent the upper end of what most hospitality and service work pays here.

A study cited by WLOS found that Asheville renters would need to earn about $21.58 per hour to comfortably afford median rent, while the estimated actual hourly wage for Asheville renters was $11.34. The city ranks seventh nationally for the size of that gap. That is not a distinction anyone was aiming for.

In January 2023, workers from Asheville's tourism industry testified before the Buncombe County Tourism Development Authority Board about the impossibility of affording housing in the city where they worked. The argument was specific: the same tourism machine that generates hotel tax revenue used to fund advertising attracting more visitors is simultaneously driving the housing costs that push those visitors' servers, bartenders, and housekeepers toward the financial margins. That tension remains unresolved.

Someone in that room must have noticed. They have not said so publicly.

A server working full-time at one of downtown's busier restaurants might clear $35,000 to $42,000 in a good year including tips. A line cook earns less. The musicians who fill the city's venues piece together income from gigs, teaching, recording sessions, and merchandise sales. A barista at one of the city's well-regarded independent coffee shops might clear $32,000 to $38,000. None of these numbers, stacked or combined, get anyone across the $60,000 threshold without a roommate, a side hustle, or an arrangement that a certified financial planner would describe as creative.

These are the people who hand you your latte, play the set you drove downtown for, and pour the fourth IPA you didn't technically need. Asheville is built on their labor. Whether it has figured out how to let them actually live here is a separate and ongoing question.

The construction workers rebuilding after Helene face the same problem in a different collar. The region needs significant labor to repair homes, infrastructure, and businesses damaged by the storm, and those jobs pay real wages, often better than service work. But even a skilled tradesperson earning $55,000 to $65,000 annually finds that the qualifying income for a median-priced home is a distant target. The workforce the region needs to rebuild itself cannot comfortably afford to live in the region they are rebuilding.

The Other Tax

Asheville has a property crime rate that the relocation brochures tend to skip over. The city's numbers run above national averages, driven primarily by theft and vehicle break-ins rather than violent crime. Downtown parking lots, trailhead parking areas, and cars left overnight in popular neighborhoods are the most reliable targets. It is not unique to Asheville, but it is more persistent here than in cities of comparable size and friendliness, which creates a certain cognitive dissonance.

The practical response most residents arrive at is simple: don't leave anything visible in a parked car. Not a bag, not a charger, not a jacket. If it looks like it might be hiding something underneath it, that's enough. Locals treat this as ambient city knowledge, the same way coastal residents learn not to leave kayaks unlocked. It does not make the city feel dangerous. It does make the glove compartment feel like a municipal suggestion rather than a storage solution.

The city has invested in downtown safety initiatives and increased patrols in high-incident areas, with results that might charitably be described as ongoing. For anyone relocating from a low-crime suburb, the adjustment in habits takes about two weeks. After that it becomes routine, the car stays empty, and the city's other qualities tend to crowd out the inconvenience fairly quickly. Consider it an informal participation fee.

The Policy Response: Slow, Contentious, and Extremely Fond of Studies

Asheville is not ignoring the housing problem. It is arguing about it in the particular way that cities argue about housing, which involves a genuine clash of values, a lot of public meetings, and outcomes that tend to be smaller than the problem requires.

In September 2024, the city released its final Affordable Housing Plan, an update to a document that had not been revised since 2015. The plan establishes a 10-year implementation roadmap built around two priorities: helping existing residents stay in Asheville and breaking down barriers to homeownership and rental affordability. It is a plan for having a plan, which is an honest description of where the city was.

The more structurally significant debate is about missing middle housing, a term for the duplexes, triplexes, townhomes, cottage courts, and accessory dwelling units that exist between a single-family house and a large apartment complex. This type of housing largely disappeared from American cities over the past 70 years as single-family zoning became the dominant regulatory model. In Asheville, two-thirds of all residential neighborhoods currently permit only single-family homes.

The city commissioned a Missing Middle Housing Study, completed in November 2023, which proposed 22 zoning changes including reduced minimum lot sizes, loosened ADU requirements, and streamlined approval for cottage courts and small multi-family buildings. The study cost $115,000 and generated a year of contentious public meetings. It was thorough, well-researched, and arrived at conclusions that any working city planner could have sketched on a napkin in about forty minutes.

Enacting those recommendations turned out to be harder than commissioning the study. What actually passed at the March 2025 council meeting, after $115,000 in consulting fees, a year of public input, and enough community meetings to qualify as a minor lifestyle, was a more limited package: changes to encourage cottage and flag lots (cottage lots are small parcels designed for compact homes clustered around shared space; flag lots sit behind other homes and connect to the street through a narrow access strip, like the handle of a flag) in residential zones and streamlined approval for large multi-family projects in transit corridors. It was, charitably, the first paragraph of the answer to a question that required several chapters.

The vote was not unanimous, and the disagreement was substantive. Council members who favored more aggressive zoning reform voted for it; members who wanted to move more cautiously on changes affecting legacy neighborhoods, particularly historically Black neighborhoods, voted against it. That concern is genuine and not to be dismissed. The tension between sufficient housing growth and protecting communities with deep roots is a real problem, not a procedural excuse.

One measure that did pass, approved in October 2025,

allows garages and other utility buildings to be converted into accessory dwelling units without requiring variance review, even if the structures do not meet current setback requirements. This matters because such variance requests had made up 42 percent of the recent caseload heard by the city's Board of Adjustment. It is a real and practical change. Its relationship to a regional housing deficit of more than 34,000 units is, mathematically speaking, best described as a beginning.

Durham, North Carolina made more aggressive zoning reforms earlier and has revised them as it learned what worked. Its median home price is now nearly $200,000 lower than Buncombe County's, despite being in the same state and serving a similar demographic mix. Asheville's housing advocates point to Durham with some regularity. Asheville's planning process proceeds at its own pace.

There is also the matter of money. The city faces a significant budget deficit in the aftermath of Hurricane Helene, which has constrained what local government can fund directly. Federal CDBG and HOME Partnership Act funds continue to support housing programs, but the gap between what housing policy can accomplish and what the market requires is not closeable through planning alone. It requires supply, and supply requires either regulatory change or direct subsidy, both of which are happening more slowly than the math demands.

The Remote Work Valve

Something shifted the affordability equation significantly around 2020, and it had nothing to do with Asheville itself. When remote work became normalized across a wide range of industries, Asheville was positioned unusually well to benefit. In 2019, about 9.4 percent of workers in the Asheville metro worked primarily from home. By 2023, that figure in Buncombe County had reached 18.7 percent.

The job application data is even more striking than the employment figures. A 2023 LinkedIn analysis found that 71.5 percent of all job applications submitted by Asheville residents were for remote or hybrid positions, the second-highest rate of any U.S. metro area, trailing only Bend, Oregon. People who live in Asheville are overwhelmingly seeking work that does not depend on what local employers pay.

What this created, practically speaking, was a new category of Asheville resident whose income comes from somewhere else entirely. A software developer working remotely for a company in Seattle. A consultant whose clients are in New York. A designer whose agency is in Chicago. These are people for whom Asheville's housing costs are high but manageable, because their salaries are pegged to markets where costs are even higher. They experience the city as a relative bargain, and they are not wrong given their specific circumstances.

The city responded by building coworking infrastructure to serve this population. THRIVE, inside the historic Grove Arcade downtown, caters directly to remote workers and freelancers. The Collider, focused on sustainability and climate-related work, regularly hosts dedicated digital nomad days. Mojo Coworking offers a more casual option, and Hatch AVL in the River Arts District targets entrepreneurs and creative professionals.

Remote work did not fix Asheville's affordability problem. For people whose income comes from local employers, it changed nothing. What it did was open a financial pathway for a growing population whose salaries are decoupled from local wages, allowing them to live here on outside earnings and participate in the city's life without depending on what the local economy pays. This has been good for Asheville's tax base and its cultural vitality. It has done relatively little to help the bartenders, musicians, and service workers who were already here when the remote workers arrived.

Remote work did not change Asheville. It changed who could afford to be here. That is a subtler thing, and in some ways a more uncomfortable one.

The Two Ashevilles

There are effectively two economic Ashevilles operating in the same city at the same time. The first runs on outside money: remote workers, retirees with investment income, second-home owners, well-compensated healthcare professionals, and tourists who descend every fall to look at leaves and eat at restaurants with six-week waitlists. This Asheville experiences the city as reasonably priced, culturally rich, and well worth what it costs.

The second Asheville runs on local wages. These are the people who cook the food, pour the beer, guide the trails, staff the hotels, make the art, and play the music. They experience the same zip codes as financially precarious, with housing costs that eat an outsized share of what local employers pay.

A bartender at one of the city's craft beer destinations and a remote software engineer sitting at the bar are neighbors in the civic sense. They share the same tap handles, the same view out the window, probably the same Spotify playlist pumping through the sound system. One of them checked their portfolio app before ordering. The other is doing mental math about whether this shift covers Thursday's rent.

The friction is not dramatic. Asheville is too friendly a city for public confrontations about income inequality, and the two populations are too interleaved in daily life to maintain clean divisions. But it shows up in the Tourism Development Authority hearings, in the housing policy debates, in the very specific look on a longtime resident's face when someone from out of town says they just love how affordable Asheville is compared to where they came from.

The core awkwardness is structural: a city whose appeal depends substantially on the people who live and work here at local wages is also a city that makes living here at local wages progressively harder. The server, the guitarist, the river guide, and the ceramicist in the River Arts District are why the place is interesting. If the cost of living eventually makes their presence optional, whatever replaces the city they built will be something blander and considerably easier to afford.

The short-term rental market adds another layer to the math. Buncombe County has seen significant growth in short-term rental registrations, with several thousand active listings on platforms like Airbnb and Vrbo pulling housing units out of the long-term rental pool. A property that might otherwise house a teacher or a line cook is instead available by the night at a rate that reflects what a visitor will pay for a fall weekend in the mountains, which is considerably more than what the local rental market will bear on a twelve-month lease. The city has debated short-term rental regulation for years, adopted rules requiring owner-occupancy in some zones, and continues to revise its approach as the market evolves. The outcome is an ongoing negotiation between two legitimate uses of the same housing stock, in a city that does not have enough of it for either.

The largest single age cohort in the city today is 30-to-34-year-olds, at roughly 9,094 residents. Between 2000 and 2016, the 20-to-34 share of the metro population grew by 17 percent. The city's median age of 40.7 years reflects the broader demographic reality: this is not a young city by the numbers, but it has a young professional population that is choosing to be here in ways that involve some genuine financial creativity.

The Music Scene Has No Business Being This Good

Living in a city with an outsized music scene means you cannot escape it, and after a while you stop trying, and then it becomes unclear whether you are a local or a permanent tourist in your own neighborhood.

On any given weekend, live music is happening simultaneously at a dozen venues across the city. For a city of 95,000, this is not normal. Most cities this size have a bar with live music on Fridays. Asheville has a scene, which is a different thing, and which comes with the social obligation to attend things whether or not you feel like it.

The financial weight of all this is worth stating plainly. From 2010 to 2018, music industry employment in Asheville grew by 76 percent, and the concentration of jobs in musical instrument manufacturing was 9.54 times the national average. The music industry contributes $171 million to the gross regional product and generates roughly $10 million annually in state and local tax revenue. These figures describe an actual economic sector that also produces, on a Wednesday evening, a world-class band playing down the street while your barista's mandatory EP plays in the background and your neighbor texts to remind you about their open studio.

The musicians who make this scene work are, economically speaking, running a small business with irregular revenue and fixed costs that do not care about their gig calendar. A working musician in Asheville pieces together income from live performance, teaching private lessons, session work at one of the city's recording studios, and merchandise. A good year might clear $40,000 to $50,000 for someone established enough to fill a room. A building year, while the audience grows and the bookings accumulate, looks considerably leaner. Asheville's music economy is real and well-documented, but it does not pay its participants the way a healthcare system or a tech company does, and the rent does not adjust for the difference.

The city has made deliberate efforts to treat the music industry as an economic sector rather than a cultural amenity. The Asheville Music Professionals organization provides networking, resources, and advocacy for working musicians navigating the business side of a creative career. The combination of performance culture and production infrastructure is rare at this city's scale and did not happen by accident.

It is, depending on your temperament, either an extraordinary gift or a mild form of exhaustion. Probably both, in alternating weeks.

The Creative Economy: Larger Than It Looks

The music scene is the most visible part of a broader creative economy that runs considerably deeper than most people expect, including some people who have been living inside it for years. In 2024, Buncombe County's creative occupations supported 9,061 jobs across 56 distinct creative industries. Total economic output from the creative sector reached $1.64 billion, generating $488 million in labor income and $157 million in tax revenues across all levels of government.

The $1.64 billion figure is, in practice, what it costs to live in a city where everyone you meet has a project. The photographer, the writer, the glassblower, the ceramicist who opens her studio on Saturdays and genuinely expects you to show up. The guitarist who just finished recording and would love your honest opinion. This is what $1.64 billion in creative output feels like from the inside: wonderful, relentless, and nearly impossible to escape on a weekend without planning several days in advance.

For a creative professional considering a move to Asheville, the density of that community has real practical value. Collaborators, clients, and audiences exist here in a way that does not exist in most comparably sized cities, and the professional relationships formed in that environment tend to be the ones that matter most over time. This is, the book notes while maintaining its posture, a reason not to move here.

What this means in practice for a working artist is that Asheville offers a community that is genuinely hard to find elsewhere, at a price that is genuinely hard to meet on what the creative economy pays locally. The ceramicist squeezing studio rent out of weekend sales, the graphic designer doing client work between painting commissions, the songwriter teaching guitar lessons on weekday afternoons: these are people who have made the math work through a combination of multiple income streams, shared housing, and a city that rewards the effort with something most creative professionals in more affordable places are quietly missing. It is an uncomfortable equation. It is also, for a specific kind of person with a specific set of priorities, the right one.

The Factor That Doesn't Fit the Spreadsheet

Any honest accounting of why people keep choosing Asheville despite the cost structure has to acknowledge the thing that resists quantification. The outdoor access surrounding the city is not a weekend amenity for most residents. It is the reason they are here. The trails, rivers, and mountain terrain function as ambient infrastructure, woven into daily life rather than held in reserve for special occasions.

Moving to a more affordable city and driving to the

mountains on weekends is not the same experience as living somewhere the mountains are already outside. Once access is simply where you are rather than somewhere you go, the calculation of what the city costs looks different.

What People Actually Do to Make It Work

The people who live in Asheville successfully, financially speaking, have generally converged on a small number of workable approaches. None of them are secrets, and none of them require unusual luck. They are just the practical adaptations that a city with this cost structure demands.

The most common is remote income. A salary pegged to a more expensive market, earned from a laptop anywhere in the city, is the single most reliable path to financial stability in Asheville. At $60,000 or above, a remote worker can live reasonably well as a single person. At $70,000 or above, they can begin to think realistically about homeownership, particularly as inventory has increased and the market has softened from its pandemic peak.

Two-income households clear the threshold more easily. Two people each earning $45,000 to $50,000, or one earning remotely and one locally, can afford shared housing comfortably and begin accumulating savings. The math on buying a home in that scenario is still challenging but not impossible over a medium time horizon, particularly if one of the incomes grows with professional development.

Healthcare is the local career track with the most reliable path to wages that compete with housing costs. Mission Hospital is the largest employer in the region and anchors an ecosystem of healthcare-related employment that reaches across the metro. A registered nurse, a physical therapist, a medical technician: these are careers that pay above the average local wage and provide the kind of stability that makes the rest of the budget math manageable.

Retirees represent a fourth pathway, and an honest chapter does not skip it. The mechanism is straightforward: sell a house in a market where prices are higher than Asheville's, which describes most of the Northeast, much of the Mid-Atlantic, coastal California, and a growing list of other places, arrive here with equity that functions as a down payment or an outright purchase, and you have stepped over the income bar without needing a local salary to do it. Someone arriving with substantial equity from a house they bought decades ago at a fraction of its current value is not competing with the barista for the same housing stock. They are operating in a different market entirely.

What draws retirees specifically, beyond the general appeal that draws everyone, is the particular combination of cultural engagement and physical accessibility that Asheville offers in unusual concentration. The food scene is world-class without requiring a flight to get there. The arts and music calendar runs year-round and skews toward quality rather than spectacle. The outdoor infrastructure accommodates people at a range of fitness levels, from serious hikers to people who want a pleasant walk with a genuinely excellent view.

The city is compact enough to be navigable without a car for many daily tasks. The climate, with four actual seasons and none of them requiring industrial-grade heating or cooling for eight months of the year, is the kind that people from the Upper Midwest mention first when explaining why they left. The retirement community infrastructure is covered in a later chapter, but the short version is that the options range from full-service campuses to active adult neighborhoods to simply buying a house and living among people of all ages, which turns out to be what a lot of retirees actually want.

None of this means retirees are immune to the math. Asheville is not cheap by any measure, and someone arriving on a fixed income without meaningful equity is looking at the same housing costs and above-average cost of living that everyone else faces. The retiree pathway works best when the equity is there, the income is sufficient, and the budget has room for a few surprises. Asheville is not a city that runs out of surprises.

Shared housing remains common among younger residents on local wages. Two or three people splitting a two-bedroom apartment can each land in the $40,000 to $45,000 range for total housing costs while still living in the city they chose. It is not a permanent solution for most people, but it is a functional one while careers develop. The social infrastructure of Asheville means that shared housing here tends to come with a quality of life that shared housing in a more affordable but less interesting city cannot match.

The plans that tend not to work involve arriving on a single local service-sector income without supplemental income or shared housing, and hoping the vibe makes it feel more affordable than the numbers suggest. Asheville's vibe is genuine and extraordinary, but it does not adjust the cost of a one-bedroom apartment. The city is not less expensive because it is beautiful. It is expensive partly because it is beautiful, which is the oldest dynamic in real estate.

The Uncomfortable Arithmetic

Asheville is a city with high cultural output, exceptional outdoor access, a food scene that punches considerably above its weight, and housing costs that are materially higher than what most local employers pay. The gap between what the city offers and what it costs to live here is real and persistent. It is narrowing in some respects, slowly and unevenly, as the market softens and policy responses accumulate. But it is not closing in ways that a person moving here next month can count on.

Anyone moving to Asheville should go in with a specific plan for bridging that gap. The plan does not have to be elegant, but it has to exist. The people who arrive with one tend to stay. The people who arrive without one tend to spend their first year making one under pressure, which is not the most enjoyable way to discover an otherwise excellent city.

The housing market, as of early 2026, is more favorable to buyers than it has been in several years. Inventory has risen to four to five months of supply, homes are sitting on the market longer, and sellers are more open to negotiation than during the competitive peaks of 2021 and 2022. The urgency that characterized the pandemic-era market has eased, and a patient, strategic buyer has more options than they would have had two years ago. The softening is most pronounced at the high end, with luxury properties over $1.5 million sitting with 20 months of inventory, while supply below $400,000 remains genuinely constrained.

Twenty months of inventory on the luxury end means a lot of sellers reconsidering their floor. Below $400,000, the word "available" is doing the work of a rumor.

What the data does not fully capture is the consistent testimony of people who worked out the math and stayed. The language they use tends to converge on the same ideas regardless of where they came from or what they do. One person described it as the only place they had moved to where they did not feel the restless need to keep moving. Another called it the most West Coast-feeling city on the East Coast. A third simply said: you sort out the career and the housing, and then everything else takes care of itself, and the everything else is better here than anywhere I've lived.

Very few people leave Asheville because they stopped loving

the place. The departure rate is driven by economics, not by disenchantment, which is a meaningful distinction. A city people leave reluctantly is a different kind of city from one people leave happily.

Asheville is expensive for what it is. It is also, for a specific and growing number of people who have worked out the math, exactly what they were looking for and worth every dollar of what it costs. The city does not resolve that contradiction. It just keeps being both things simultaneously, and leaving people to decide for themselves which side of it they want to be on.

CHAPTER FOUR

DON'T MOVE HERE
IF YOU HATE THE OUTDOORS

There are cities where nature is a destination. You schedule it. You pack the bag, check the weather, load snacks into a cooler, consult a parking app, and commit a meaningful portion of a weekend to getting somewhere green. Asheville, North Carolina is not one of those cities.

In Asheville, nature is not a destination. It is a condition. It is the ambient fact of where you live. It is the red-tailed hawk riding thermals above Merrimon Avenue on a Tuesday morning. It is the bear that knocked over your neighbor's compost bin sometime around 3 a.m. It is the ridge of blue mountains that fills your windshield every single time you look up from a stoplight. If you are the kind of person who considers "the outdoors" to be the inconvenient gap between your front door and your car, you need to know what you are getting into.

Black bears in Western North Carolina are not the dramatic, tourist-brochure bears of Yellowstone. They are not standing in rivers catching salmon. They are not surveying the horizon from a rocky promontory. They are in your neighbor's trash at 2 a.m. on a Tuesday, methodically working through last week's leftovers with the focused efficiency of someone who has done this before and will do it again. Buncombe County is home to one of the densest black bear populations in the eastern United States, and the bears have correctly identified residential garbage as a reliable food source that requires considerably less effort than foraging. They are not aggressive. They are not particularly impressed by you, either. The standard encounter goes like this: you hear something outside, you turn on the porch light, a bear the size of a loveseat looks up from your recycling bin, holds eye contact for a moment longer than is comfortable, and then goes back to what it was doing. You are an inconvenience. The bin is the point. Welcome to the neighborhood. The mountains are beautiful, by the way. You will notice them once you get the bin back inside.

The bears, for their part, have excellent taste in real estate. Within forty-five minutes of downtown Asheville, you can stand on the highest peak east of the Mississippi River. You can hike a section of the most famous long-distance trail on the continent. You can slide sixty feet down a natural rock waterslide into a cold mountain pool. You can cast a fly line into one of the hundred best trout streams in the country. You can paddle Class IV whitewater through the deepest gorge east of the Mississippi. You can do all of that on a Saturday and still make your dinner reservation at 7.

That last sentence is technically true. Nobody said anything about Sunday.

Sunday, if we are being honest, is when the reality of living in a place this beautiful and this expensive catches up with you. The mortgage or the rent on the house that gives you that mountain view was not free. The car that makes the forty-five-minute drive possible requires insurance, gas, and the kind of maintenance that keeps pace with mountain roads rather than flat ones. The gear accumulates. The waders, the bike, the trail shoes, the layers for the cold, the layers for the warm, the dry bags for the river, the chalk bag for the crag: all of it costs money, and none of it buys itself. Asheville is a city that sells proximity to wilderness at a premium, and the premium is real. You are not just buying a house. You are paying for the right to live near 1.1 million acres of federally protected land, most of which you will drive past on the way to a brewery and feel good about theoretically.

And then there is winter.

Not the postcard winter. Not the version with the frost on the Blue Ridge Parkway and the snow-dusted spruce trees and the hot coffee at the summit overlook. The real winter, which runs from roughly December through March and can be accurately described as the absolute drizzled shits. It is not cold enough to be dramatic. It is not warm enough to be comfortable. It is forty-one degrees and raining sideways on a Tuesday, and the trail you planned to hike is a mud channel, and the Parkway has been closed since Thursday due to ice, and you are sitting inside your beautiful mountain-view house in two sweatshirts eating soup and watching the fog consume the ridge you can usually see from the kitchen window.

This is nature as ambient condition. It is ambient in all directions.

The honest version of the Saturday test is that it requires a Saturday in which you are not tired, not busy, not deterred by the forecast, not behind on laundry, not waiting for a delivery, and not still processing the previous Saturday's mileage in your knees. Some weeks, all of those conditions align and you go. Some weeks, you get home from work on Friday, look at the 1.1 million acres available to you, and decide that tonight the acres can manage themselves. You will pour something reasonable, sit in the chair by the window, and watch the mountains do their thing from a respectful distance.

The mountains do not take it personally. They have been there for 480 million years. They can wait until you feel like it.

Spend any time talking to people who moved to Asheville from a major metro area and a pattern emerges. They all describe a version of the same experience: the first time they drove forty minutes and found themselves standing at a waterfall, or on a ridge with a hundred-mile view, they pulled out their phone to share it and then put it away again because no photograph was going to work. The place requires being in it.

Even when you are too tired to be in it. Even when it is forty-one degrees and raining. Even when the Parkway is closed and the trail is mud and the couch has made a compelling counter-argument. The knowledge that it is out there, available on a day when you are ready, turns out to be its own form of wealth.

A form that does not, unfortunately, offset the rent.

The Numbers Do Not Seem Real Until You Live Here

Start with a simple inventory and you will understand why people who move here from other places develop a slightly glazed look when they try to describe it to friends back home.

Pisgah National Forest wraps around Asheville on multiple sides, and the nearest trailhead is less than ten minutes from downtown. Not ten minutes from the edge of the metro area. Ten minutes from the center of the city. The trail network across all three ranger districts exceeds a thousand miles of hiking, mountain biking, and horseback riding trails.

This is a federal forest, not a park. There are no entrance fees. You just drive in, which means there is nothing stopping you from doing exactly that on a weeknight after dinner, which is a sentence that will rearrange your sense of what evenings are for.

Then there is Nantahala National Forest, the largest national forest in North Carolina, anchoring the southwestern corner of the state. Together, Pisgah and Nantahala comprise more than 1.1 million acres of federally protected mountain land, covering more ground than the entire state of Rhode Island. Asheville sits at the center of it, not on the edge of it, the way a raisin ends up in the middle of a muffin without anyone planning it that way.

From there, keep adding. Great Smoky Mountains National Park is about an hour south. DuPont State Recreational Forest is less than 50 minutes out. Chimney Rock State Park is 25 miles from downtown.

Gorges State Park, with its 26 waterfalls and more annual rainfall than the Pacific Northwest, is about 55 miles out. At some point the map becomes a solid block of green and you stop adding pins.

The list genuinely does not stop. At some point you give up cataloging it and just accept that you live somewhere unusual. Other cities have a park. Asheville has a biome.

The Blue Ridge Parkway: Sixteen Million People Cannot Be Wrong

If you ask most people what the most visited unit of the entire National Park System is, they will guess Yellowstone or the Grand Canyon. They will be wrong. The answer is the Blue Ridge Parkway, and it is not particularly close.

The Parkway stretches 469 miles from Shenandoah National Park in Virginia to Great Smoky Mountains National Park in North Carolina, with 252 of those miles running through North Carolina specifically. In 2025, the National Park Service confirmed 16.5 million visits, keeping it at the top of the entire National Park System despite Hurricane Helene having closed major sections during peak fall 2024. The storm wiped out two-thirds of the Parkway's October traffic in a single season. The road lost the peak of leaf season and still finished first. On a Sunday in mid-October, you will feel every single one of those visitors.

From most neighborhoods in Asheville, you can be on the Parkway in fifteen minutes. Not near it. On it.

The Parkway contains 300 miles of hiking trails, eight campgrounds, and thirteen picnic areas, and it slices through terrain that would individually serve as a signature regional attraction anywhere else. Here the overlooks are just mile markers you pass on your way to the next one. Elevations range from 600 feet to over 6,000 feet. The section nearest Asheville passes Craggy Gardens, skirts Mount Mitchell, crosses the French Broad River valley, and winds south through scenery that fills more camera rolls than any other stretch of road in the eastern United States.

Built during the Depression era in the 1930s to put people to work and pump money into struggling mountain communities, the Parkway succeeded in ways its planners could never have anticipated. It was originally conceived as a route connecting two national parks rather than a destination in its own right, which is one of those planning miscalculations that worked out extremely well for everyone except local traffic.

The Parkway changes character through the seasons. Spring brings rhododendron blooms that carpet the roadsides from May through June. Craggy Gardens, about 20 minutes from Asheville at Mile 364, sits at 5,500 feet and the Catawba rhododendron there does not bloom so much as erupt. In June, you walk into a tunnel of tangled, dripping shrubs ten feet overhead, the air cold and wet even when the valley below is warm, the color so saturated that it looks like someone turned the saturation dial past the point of realism.

Fall turns the ridgelines every shade between gold and burgundy, peaking in mid-October at higher elevations. Winter closes some sections but leaves others passable, and the snowfall on the exposed meadows at Black Balsam Knob, which sits above treeline at nearly 6,000 feet with nothing between you and the wind for 360 degrees, looks like somewhere considerably more remote than 25 miles from a brewpub.

One practical note before you start planning your first drive: the Parkway is not always open. Sections close for weather, rockslides, construction, and the occasional ice event that arrives without much warning. Before you head out, check the official road closure page at nps.gov/blri to confirm your intended stretch is passable. It takes thirty seconds and saves a U-turn at a locked gate.

You can resent the Parkway's existence on a summer weekend afternoon, when the overlooks fill up and the speeds drop, and that is fair. From the moment the first settlers drove livestock down these mountain roads to the markets in the piedmont, traffic in this region has been a problem of abundance. The livestock have been replaced by out-of-state Subarus riding their brakes down 6,000-foot grades, but the fundamental dynamic has not changed. There are more people who want to use this road than the road can comfortably absorb. The reason for that is the road.

The Appalachian Trail Is Technically Accessible by Afternoon

Most Americans think of the Appalachian Trail as a bucket-list undertaking. A 2,197-mile odyssey from Springer Mountain in Georgia to Mount Katahdin in Maine, requiring months, strong knees, and a tolerance for sleeping on the ground next to strangers. For people who live in Asheville, it is a day trip option.

The AT travels 95.7 miles through North Carolina proper, plus an additional 224 miles along the North Carolina-Tennessee border, with summits that reach above 6,000 feet. Multiple trailheads are within an hour's drive of downtown. The Mountains-to-Sea Trail, a 935-mile North Carolina route stretching from Clingmans Dome to the Outer Banks, crosses Craven Gap just fifteen minutes from the city center.

The town of Hot Springs, where the Appalachian Trail passes directly through the center of town past the post office and the general store, is just 35 miles northwest of Asheville. It is one of the only places on the entire 2,197-mile trail where you can walk through a real community's main street with a pack on your back, pick up a resupply, and keep moving. For Asheville residents it is a short Sunday drive. For thru-hikers it is a landmark moment. The town takes both with equal calm.

Max Patch, a grassy, treeless summit in the Pisgah National Forest that the AT crosses at 4,629 feet, offers 360-degree panoramic views that show up on every list of best day hikes in the Southeast. On a clear autumn weekend it is genuinely crowded, because word got out some years ago and has not been walking back. If you want the view to yourself, go on a Tuesday in February and dress accordingly.

Roan Mountain, along the North Carolina-Tennessee border, forms the largest stretch of natural grassy balds in the southern Appalachians, covering over 600 acres of open ridgeline above 6,000 feet. In late June, the Catawba rhododendron bloom turns the high meadows a shade of purple that looks edited. Photographers travel from several states away to capture it. Asheville residents drive 90 minutes, take a walk, eat a sandwich on a boulder, and drive home in time for dinner. It is one of those situations where proximity turns a genuine wonder into an errand.

This is the tragedy of living here: you will treat the Appalachian Trail like a dog park. Not metaphorically. Literally. You will say "I'm going to walk a piece of the AT this weekend" with the same energy most people reserve for "I'm going to grab some groceries." The 2,197-mile trail that people take six months off work to complete, the one that appears on bucket lists and documentary films and the kind of social media posts that get two hundred comments, will become your Tuesday afternoon option.

You will complete a section of it while listening to a podcast. You will come home with mud on your boots and describe the experience as "nice." Somewhere, a thru-hiker who just walked 800 miles to reach the same ridge is weeping and does not know why.

300 Waterfalls Within Two Hours. Some Before Breakfast.

Western North Carolina contains more waterfalls per square mile than almost anywhere else in the eastern United States, and at some point geological modesty went out the window entirely. The region did not choose this. The geology simply arranged itself this way, and now everyone has to deal with it.

Transylvania County, sitting just south of Asheville, officially calls itself the Land of Waterfalls and backs that claim with 250 documented falls within its borders. A comprehensive map of Western North Carolina waterfalls tracks over 300 named falls across the region. The variety runs from roadside spectacles that require no more effort than parking to serious backcountry hikes through terrain that will test your judgment and your knees.

Looking Glass Falls in Pisgah National Forest drops 60 feet

into a wide pool, and you can see it from the road. You park, walk down a short flight of stone steps, and you are standing at the base with the creek churning at your feet and the mist cooling your face. The drive from Asheville takes about 35 minutes and requires roughly the same logistical effort as a trip to the pharmacy, which is either wonderful or the beginning of a problem depending on your schedule.

And then there is Sliding Rock. If you have never heard of Sliding Rock, here is what it is: a smooth 60-foot natural rock waterslide where the creek delivers 11,000 gallons per minute into a deep, cold pool at the bottom. The water is moving very fast and it is not warm. The Forest Service has lifeguards on duty in summer, which tells you something about how this usually goes. The drive from Asheville is about 45 minutes.

What the trailhead maps do not fully prepare you for is the line. On a summer weekend, families who have been making this drive annually since the 1970s arrive early. Grandparents who slid down this same rock as children now watch grandchildren take the plunge, screaming, into that freezing pool with the specific joy of someone who knows exactly what is about to happen to someone they love. You will wait your turn in the sun, sunburning gently through a t-shirt, watching stranger after stranger get launched off the same smooth granite face at a speed that always looks faster than expected, followed immediately by the same expression of shock that nobody ever manages to suppress.

When you finally reach the top, the cold of the water is not a temperature. It is a physical event. It removes your breath. It removes several thoughts you were having. The pool at the bottom is significantly deeper and significantly colder than any reasonable preparation could have led you to expect, and you will surface gasping, wade to the edge, and stand dripping on a rock thinking about going again.

You will go again. This is not optional. This is the ritual. The mountain has been running it for decades and nobody has ever successfully resisted the second slide.

The rest of the region's waterfall inventory includes cascades tall enough to generate their own weather, remote enough to require genuine effort, and varied enough that locals develop strong opinions about which ones are overrated. There are waterfalls in this region that drop hundreds of feet and most people in Asheville could not tell you their names off the top of their heads. That level of embarrassment of riches is the whole point.

After a while, you stop being surprised by the waterfalls. You just note them the way you note good street parking. Which is perhaps the most honest sentence about life in Western North Carolina that this chapter contains.

The French Broad River: Ancient, Stubborn, and Running Through Your City

The French Broad River flows through Asheville, threading the River Arts District and the city's industrial corridor before heading north. On any afternoon you can stand on a pedestrian bridge and watch kayakers work through a rapid while herons stand motionless in the shallows twenty feet away. This river has been doing something more or less like this for an extraordinarily long time. Longer, it turns out, than the mountains it flows through.

Geological estimates place the French Broad among the oldest rivers in the world, with current scientific assessments putting it at between 300 and 340 million years old. To understand what this means in practical terms: the river predates the Appalachian Mountains. It was already flowing through this landscape when the mountains rose around it. A younger river, faced with a new mountain range, would have rerouted.

The French Broad declined to do that. It kept its course and carved deeper, which is why you now drive through a river valley rather than over a ridge. The river won. The mountains just grew up around it and eventually accepted the situation.

This stubbornness deserves a moment of appreciation, because it is a genuinely strange geological story. The Appalachian Mountains are themselves ancient, forming around 480 million years ago and ranking among the oldest mountain ranges on Earth. The French Broad predates the most recent mountain-building event by roughly 150 to 200 million years. It was already well-established when the latest round of mountains arrived. It had been flowing through that landscape long enough to have a routine, and when the earth buckled and heaved and tried to change the route, the river just kept cutting downward, a little deeper every thousand centuries, until the mountains had no choice but to work around it.

There is a word for this kind of river: antecedent, meaning one that predates the landscape it flows through. There are not many of them. The French Broad is one of the most dramatic examples in the world, and it runs through the middle of a mid-sized city where people are trying to park.

This is either an inspiring geological story about persistence or a slightly unsettling reminder that the river has been here incomparably longer than anyone currently living along its banks, and will be here after every trace of us is gone. Either way, the kayakers seem to be enjoying themselves. Some of them are reading books in inner tubes. The river is somewhere between 300 and 340 million years old, has survived the rise and erosion of an entire mountain range, and is too old to be offended by a person floating down it with a paperback novel. It has seen worse.

Today the French Broad carries kayakers, tubers, stand-up

paddleboarders, fly anglers, and the occasional person who just wants to float in an inner tube and read a book while the current handles the navigation. Outfitters launch trips from locations 30 minutes from downtown, with options ranging from calm flatwater floats past the Biltmore Estate to full-day whitewater runs through Class II to Class IV rapids. The river keeps getting discovered by the outdoor press, which publishes enthusiastic articles about it with some regularity, which means the secret is somewhat out, which means you can expect company. This is the consequence of living inside a river basin surrounded by steep mountains that funnel cold water downhill at interesting speeds.

But the French Broad is just the start. The Nantahala River, whose name comes from the Cherokee phrase meaning "land of the noonday sun" because the gorge is so deep it only receives direct sunlight at midday, offers eight miles of rapids and has introduced more first-time paddlers to whitewater than perhaps any other river in the Southeast. The Nolichucky, about 45 minutes from Asheville, cuts through one of the deepest river gorges east of the Mississippi. The Tuckasegee, the North Toe, and sections of the Pigeon River complete a menu covering every level from lazy float to committed technical paddling within a reasonable drive of downtown.

The French Broad River Park on the south side of the city and the greenway system connecting it to Carrier Park give residents a continuous stretch of river access that is walkable, bikeable, and woven into the daily life of the city in a way that now feels inevitable. You can walk to the river from a significant portion of Asheville's south side neighborhoods. In summer, many people do exactly that after work and consider the day improved.

If you do not like rivers, this is the part where you start

wondering whether Asheville is going to be expensive for the amount of landscape you are choosing to ignore.

Over 4,000 Miles of Trout Streams. Trout Unlimited Is Paying Attention.

Western North Carolina contains more than 4,000 miles of trout streams. That number is large enough that it loses meaning quickly, so here is a different way to think about it: if you drove every mile of trout stream in this region at highway speed, it would take you the better part of three days to reach the end. And you would pass through land-scapes of cold, clear mountain water the entire way.

This is, objectively, too many trout streams. Nobody needs 4,000 miles of trout streams. It is the kind of excess that produces a specific type of person who moves here from somewhere without mountains, discovers that the creeks run cold and clear within twenty minutes of downtown, and quietly begins spending weekends standing in them. Within a year they own waders. Within two, they have developed opinions about fly patterns and are explaining them to people who did not ask.

The region also has stocked tailwaters for people who just want to catch something and eat lunch by a creek without investing in a philosophy. Both approaches coexist peace-fully. The philosophical ones haunt the smaller, higher-elevation headwater creeks after wild fish that have never seen a hatchery and do not make things easy. The pragmatic ones park at a pull-off and do just fine.

What nobody warns you about is the gear. Fly fishing has developed an entire costuming tradition that has very little to do with catching fish and everything to do with looking like someone who catches fish. The waders alone run several hundred dollars. The rod is another several hundred. The vest, the net, the forceps, the nippers, the tippet spools, the fly boxes with their hand-tied contents representing dozens of hours of someone's evenings, the wool hat, the polarized sunglasses: by the time you are standing in a creek outside Brevard, you have spent close to a thousand dollars to outsmart a creature with a brain roughly the size of a pea.

The trout is not impressed. The trout does not know you exist. The trout is doing what it has always done, finning in the current, and you are the newcomer here by a margin of several hundred million years.

Wilson Creek, designated a Wild and Scenic River about an hour east of Asheville, runs cold and clear through a remote gorge with native brook trout in its upper sections. These fish are wild and self-sustaining, which matters enormously to the people who care about such things and means nothing to the river, which does not track human distinctions between wild and stocked. Sections of Wilson Creek also include serious whitewater, which means the same watershed rewards both anglers and paddlers, sometimes within sight of each other, each quietly convinced their use of the creek is the correct one.

Mount Mitchell: The Highest Point East of the Mississippi, 35 Miles Away

Mount Mitchell reaches 6,684 feet above sea level, making it the highest point in the Appalachian Mountains and the highest peak east of the Mississippi River. It is located in Mount Mitchell State Park, 35 miles northeast of downtown Asheville via the Blue Ridge Parkway. You can drive most of the way to the summit on a paved road. On a clear day, the observation platform at the top provides views stretching roughly 85 miles in every direction. This is not a reasonable thing for a city of this size to have access to, and yet here we are.

The summit is typically 15 to 20 degrees cooler than downtown Asheville on any given day. In summer, when the city sits at 80 degrees and the humidity reminds you that you are technically in the South, the summit of Mount Mitchell can be 60 degrees and breezy. On many days you drive up through the cloud layer and emerge above it, looking down at a white ceiling with mountain peaks poking through. This particular view is available to Asheville residents on a long lunch break.

Mount Craig, at 6,647 feet, stands just north of Mitchell on the same ridge and is the second-highest peak east of the Mississippi. Most hikers connect the two on the same outing via the 2.1-mile ridge trail between them. The ridge is a high-elevation spruce-fir forest that smells like the far north and feels like it: cool, dim, quiet, with the particular silence of a landscape too high and cold for most of what grows at lower elevations. First-time visitors from the Southeast sometimes stop and say it does not feel like North Carolina, and they are correct. It does not.

Asheville residents refer to going up to Mount Mitchell the way people in other cities refer to running errands. It is on the way to nothing in particular, and it is available whenever the weather looks good and the mood strikes. You should probably check the forecast before you go, because the summit is the kind of place that can be sunny and warm at 9 a.m. and actively unpleasant by noon, and the clouds do not send advance notice.

Linville Gorge: Something a National Park Ought to Have Claimed

About 60 miles northeast of Asheville, the land drops without warning. Linville Gorge is a 12-mile canyon that plunges 2,000 feet to the Linville River below, forming what is regularly described as the Grand Canyon of the East. The comparison understates the experience. The Grand

Canyon is wide and horizontal. Linville Gorge is vertical, claustrophobic in places, and the kind of terrain that reminds you that "wilderness area" is a designation with actual meaning.

The Linville Gorge Wilderness Area encompasses nearly 12,000 acres within Pisgah National Forest and contains 39 miles of trails. The area was largely spared from the clear-cutting that stripped much of the southern Appalachians in the late 19th and early 20th centuries, so the gorge retains some of the best old-growth forest in the region. On the canyon floor, beside the river, the trees are old enough and the rock walls close enough overhead that the place develops its own microclimate and its own rules.

The Cherokee called it "Eseeoh," meaning a river of many cliffs, which is accurate to the point of understatement. The cliffs are not decorative. West rim paths drop sharply. East rim routes climb to overlooks at Table Rock and Hawksbill Mountain where the view down the gorge stops your forward progress entirely until you consciously decide to keep moving. The Linville Gorge Trail runs 11.5 miles along the river at the bottom, where the canyon walls rise on both sides and the sense of scale is something photographs cannot convey. Your forearms start to feel the exposure before your brain has finished processing what you are looking at.

Linville Falls, accessible directly from the Blue Ridge Parkway at the gorge's northern end, drops roughly 90 feet over multiple levels before the water enters the gorge. Five separate viewpoints on different parts of the trail system give you the upper falls, the lower falls from below, and the narrow flume where the river funnels between rock walls before the canyon opens. The trailhead draws casual Parkway visitors. The gorge itself, beginning a short distance in either direction, is something else entirely.

Linville Gorge is the kind of place that makes people who

grew up in the mountains take it slightly for granted, which is the highest compliment a landscape can receive.

Mountain Biking: Pisgah Trails Have a National Reputation For a Reason

Asheville has developed a quiet reputation in the mountain biking world that is no longer particularly quiet. The trails in and around Pisgah National Forest are discussed in the same breath as Moab and Bentonville, and riders from across the country plan trips specifically around them. If you ride a bike and you move here, understand what you are walking into financially, socially, and physically before you unpack.

Pisgah National Forest contains approximately 485 miles of mountain biking trails across all difficulty levels. The classic Pisgah riding experience involves chunky rock gardens, root-choked singletrack through dark hemlock hollows, creek crossings that will get your feet wet regardless of what you tell yourself beforehand, and descents that reward technical skill and punish inattention with specific, immediate honesty. Trails like Black Mountain, Bennett Gap, and the Avery Creek network are revered by riders who prefer their mountain biking to feel like it was designed by the mountain rather than for the mountain. There is a difference, and Pisgah is firmly on one side of it.

The financial consequences of living near this terrain escalate faster than most people plan for. The entry-level hardtail that served you perfectly well in your previous city will last approximately one ride before the terrain makes clear that you need more suspension, better brakes, and shoes that drain faster. Full-suspension bikes capable of handling the upper tiers of Pisgah singletrack start at three thousand dollars and climb from there into territory that polite company does not discuss at dinner. Most Asheville cyclists who arrived without serious gear have upgraded within eighteen months.

This is not peer pressure. This is the terrain informing you of its requirements.

The physical toll is less discussed but equally real. The terrain does not care how fit you are when you arrive. The first time you attempt Black Mountain Trail on a warm September afternoon, you will discover muscles you had no previous reason to develop, because your previous city did not have a sustained 2,500-foot climb over loose, rooted, rocky singletrack followed by a descent that requires active, continuous decisions every thirty feet.

You will make it back to the car. You will sit in the parking lot for a few minutes. You will feel it for three days. And you will go back, because this is what living here does to otherwise reasonable people.

For those who want to ride without driving 30 minutes first, Bent Creek Experimental Forest is seven minutes from Asheville and offers 54 miles of trails across 55 routes. Kolo Bike Park, within city limits, provides 24 dedicated trails for progression and repeat laps. The proximity is the point: you can change into kit, drive seven minutes, ride for two hours, and be back before dinner gets cold. And then you will tell people about the ride at dinner. And then your non-cycling friends will slowly stop inviting you to Saturday morning things, because every Saturday morning you are already somewhere in the forest, and you were not apologetic about it the last three times they asked.

DuPont State Forest contributes another 90 miles of multiuse trails with a different character than Pisgah's more demanding terrain, offering riding that appeals to a broader range of people. In a single county, you can find beginner fire roads, technical riding through mossy hollows, bike park features, and expert terrain that requires both skill and nerve, within a reasonable drive of each other. This variety is not common. Most riding regions have a character. This one has several, and they will all eventually cost you something.

Skiing Is Closer Than You Think It Has Any Right to Be

Nobody relocates to Asheville for the skiing. That is an honest statement and not a knock on the skiing. The Southern Appalachians are not the Rockies, and pretending otherwise would be unkind to everyone involved. What skiing exists within an easy drive of Asheville offers a specific and honest experience: it is accessible, it is convenient, and it is better than sitting inside watching the weather forecast.

Hatley Pointe Ski Resort, formerly known as Wolf Ridge, is located near Mars Hill, roughly 30 minutes from downtown Asheville. It has undergone substantial renovation in recent years aimed at a more upscale mountain experience, which in ski resort terms means the lift tickets have been priced accordingly. It is the closest ski area to Asheville and the one most likely to see local vehicles in the lot on a weekday afternoon when the conditions are right.

Cataloochee Ski Area in Maggie Valley has been running lifts long enough that the skiers who came as children now bring their own children, which is either heartwarming or a sign that the mountain has been quietly building a captive audience for sixty-plus years. Sugar Mountain, about 90 minutes north, and Beech Mountain, roughly two hours out, round out the options. Between them, on a good January weekend, you can find a legitimate ski day without booking a flight, which is not nothing.

The season typically runs from late November or early December through March, weather depending. Most years deliver at least a few weeks of genuinely good conditions between natural snowfall and snowmaking. Nobody is suggesting you move here for the skiing. But the ability to wake up on a Thursday in January, drive 30 minutes, ski for three hours, and be back in your neighborhood for lunch is a quality-of-life detail that compounds quietly over years of living here.

Rock Climbing From Beginner Problems to Multi-Pitch Trad Routes

The climbing landscape around Asheville covers more ground than most people plan for. This is the nature of the region's outdoor problem generally: you come for one thing and discover three others you were not expecting. Climbers who move here for the sport tend to develop an expanding list of crags they have not gotten to yet, which is a pleasant form of being perpetually behind.

Rumbling Bald, located near Lake Lure southeast of Asheville, offers over 500 routes across traditional climbing, sport climbing, and bouldering disciplines. The grades run the full spectrum from entry-level problems to routes that will humble experienced climbers. The setting above the lake means that on a good Saturday the parking lot fills early, the crags smell like chalk, and the sound of people working problems they cannot quite crack yet drifts up from the boulders below the main wall. Bring a jacket for the shaded routes even on warm days.

Looking Glass Rock, a massive granite dome in Pisgah National Forest about an hour from Asheville, is not a place to arrive at casually. The sheer face and crack systems draw climbers from across the Southeast, the approach is a hike, the descent requires a working knowledge of what you are doing, and the exposure on the upper pitches will clarify quickly whether you have overstated your experience level. Climbers who know what they are doing love it. Climbers who misjudged the situation also love it, eventually, once the drive home has given them perspective.

Black Mountain Crag, a short drive east of Asheville near the town of Black Mountain, requires a short walk from the parking area, which is the kind of sentence that sounds like nothing until you realize it means locals are climbing there after work on a Tuesday. Table Rock and Shortoff Mountain in Linville Gorge add further options for committed climbers willing to make the drive north. The problem with the climbing around Asheville is not that it runs out. It does not run out. The problem is that it keeps expanding your list of places you have not been yet, which is exactly the kind of problem the rest of this chapter has been describing.

The Thing About All of This

Here is the thing about all of this: the real story is not any single piece of it.

Most American cities take justified pride in one significant piece of outdoor access. A national forest within reasonable distance. A river running through downtown. A park system worth mentioning. One of these things would be the defining outdoor characteristic of a city, the thing that goes in the brochure and gets talked about at chamber of commerce meetings.

Asheville has all of them. Simultaneously. Within arm's reach.

The most visited scenic drive in the National Park System starts fifteen minutes from downtown. The highest peak east of the Mississippi is 35 miles away. One of the oldest rivers in the world flows through the city's industrial district. Three hundred waterfalls are within a two-hour drive. There are 4,000 miles of trout streams, 485 miles of mountain biking trails in one forest, ski slopes within 30 minutes, the Appalachian Trail accessible for a day hike, and the deepest gorge on this side of the country less than two hours away.

The cumulative effect of living with all of this nearby is not immediately obvious. It does not hit you the first week. What happens over months and years is that your baseline shifts. A 45-minute drive to an extraordinary waterfall starts to feel routine. Standing on a ridge at 5,000 feet on a Wednesday morning before work becomes a thing that is technically possible and occasionally happens.

Your sense of what qualifies as remarkable outdoor access gets recalibrated upward, and it does not go back down.

What this produces, over time, is a specific kind of person: someone who will miss brunch because of a quick hike. You know this person. You may become this person.

The quick hike starts reasonably enough, maybe an hour on the Mountains-to-Sea Trail before meeting friends at 1:00. But the trail looks inviting past the first junction, and there was no cell signal to check the time, and the elevation gain was steeper than the map suggested, and then there was a waterfall, because there is always a waterfall, and now it is 4:30 and you are sending a text from the parking lot explaining that you are sorry, you lost track of time, you were in the mountains, and you will be at the brewery in forty-five minutes wearing what appears to be most of Pisgah on your boots. This is not a cautionary tale. This is a Tuesday.

This is the danger the chapter title is warning you about. Not that the outdoors here is bad. Not even that it is overwhelming, though it can be. The danger is that you will develop a completely distorted sense of normal, and then if life ever takes you somewhere else, you will spend months being quietly baffled by the absence of it all.

People who move away from Asheville talk about missing the mountains the way people talk about missing a person.

There is specificity to it. Not mountains in general. These mountains. This ridge. The way the fog sits in the valley on a cold November morning. The specific shade of blue the Smokies turn in late afternoon. The fact that your commute to work gave you a mountain view every single day and you only really noticed it on the days when clouds blocked it.

Locals call it being ruined for other places. It is not said with arrogance. It is said with the mild resignation of someone who tried living somewhere flatter and found the experience continuously nagging. The mountains become a reference point you did not know you were building until it is gone, and once you know it is possible to live with all of this within reach, the absence of it registers in a way you cannot fully explain to someone who has not felt it.

The outdoor access in Asheville is not a feature. It is a chronic condition of the place that gradually becomes indistinguishable from the quality of the air, the rhythm of the seasons, and the reason your neighbor cannot make brunch because they are doing a quick hike.

That quick hike ends at a waterfall. It always does.

CHAPTER FIVE

DON'T MOVE HERE
IF YOU LIKE
PREDICTABLE WEATHER

Asheville sits at 2,134 feet above sea level, and from that perch in the Blue Ridge Mountains, it does whatever it wants, whenever it wants, and without consulting anyone.

In July, the temperature on a Tuesday might be 84 degrees with low humidity and a breeze coming off the ridge. On Wednesday it rains. Thursday is glorious again. You will not know what to wear, and that is entirely the point.

People who prefer their weather neat and consistent, people who want every August to feel exactly like the last August, will find Asheville exhausting. The city's climate refuses to be summarized. It has moods. It has opinions. It surprises you in October and occasionally embarrasses you in March, when you've already put your coat away.

Here is the thing about those surprises, though. Taken all together, in any honest accounting, Asheville's climate is one of the most genuinely livable in the eastern United States. Not perfect. Not predictable. But livable in the deepest sense: climate that makes you want to spend time outside, that gives you four actual seasons, that spares you the punishing extremes that make large parts of the South and the Mountain West feel like endurance tests six months out of twelve.

This chapter is, technically, a warning. Consider yourself warned.

The Elevation Explanation

The most important thing to understand about Asheville's weather can be expressed in a single number: 2,134. That's the city's elevation in feet above sea level, and it changes everything.

At 2,134 feet, Asheville simply runs perpetually cooler than the cities at lower elevations surrounding it. The physics are straightforward enough that you don't need a textbook to feel them.

Charlotte sits at 758 feet. Atlanta is at a similar low elevation. Both cities endure July and August heat that would make a reasonable person question their choices. Asheville, meanwhile, averages a July high of 85 degrees Fahrenheit, roughly 7 to 10 degrees cooler than those cities on the same afternoon.

Seven degrees sounds modest until you've lived in both places. It's the difference between going outside and not going outside. It's the difference between running errands in the afternoon and waiting until evening. It's the difference between sleeping with the windows open and surrendering to central air.

Charlotte averages roughly 35 to 49 days per year above 90 degrees, a number that has crept steadily upward over recent decades. Atlanta is similar. In 2019, Charlotte logged 85 days at or above 90 degrees, and Atlanta exceeded 91. Asheville, in a typical year, sees about 16 days above 90 degrees. Most years, the city never reaches 100.

The mountains amplify this advantage. The Blue Ridge acts as a physical barrier, blocking warm, humid air masses that would otherwise push straight through. The vast surrounding forests cool the air through evapotranspiration, releasing water vapor that naturally lowers temperatures. It is, as someone once described it, the world's largest air conditioning system. It runs on trees and costs nothing.

None of this means Asheville is cool all summer. It is not. July is warm, humidity builds, and there are days that feel genuinely hot. But they pass. They're punctuated by rain. The evenings cool down into the mid-60s, which means you can sleep with the windows open even in the warmest months, something that large portions of the South cannot offer.

What You Actually Get, Month by Month

The annual average temperature is 56.5 degrees Fahrenheit. That number is meaningless without context, so here is the context.

January and February are the coldest months. January brings average highs around 47 degrees and lows near 28. It feels like winter without feeling punishing. You'll see freezing overnight temperatures on roughly 20 mornings in January and 16 in February. This is the season for fireplaces, wool sweaters, and the spare beauty of bare hardwoods against a mountain backdrop. March and April are where Asheville starts playing games. March highs reach the upper 50s, and April can deliver afternoons that feel like full summer, 70-degree days with warm sun and blooming redbuds everywhere. Then a front comes through and the overnight drops to 32. Gardeners in Asheville develop a particular kind of patience that is somewhere between wisdom and stubbornness.

May and June are the real transition. May highs average 75 to 77 degrees, and by June you're in the low 80s. Humidity builds, but relative to the sauna conditions in the Piedmont and the Deep South, it stays manageable. Long-time residents describe Asheville as the least humid part of North Carolina, which sounds like faint praise until you've spent a July in Raleigh. July and August are the warmest months, with highs averaging 85 and 84 degrees respectively. Evenings cool to the mid-60s. Compare that to Charlotte, where July lows hover around 70 to 71 degrees, or Atlanta, where August nights barely drop below 71. That difference in overnight temperature is one of Asheville's most under-appreciated assets.

September begins the exhale. Highs drop to the upper 70s, evenings get crisp, and something changes in the quality of light. People who've lived here long enough start watching the mountains in late September the way birders watch feeders. October and November are the headliners, and we'll get to those shortly. December brings highs near 49 and lows around 30, cold but rarely punishing, and snow is possible but far from guaranteed.

The Summer Advantage, Stated Plainly

People have been coming to these mountains to escape Southern heat for well over a century. Before air conditioning existed, the wealthy families of Charleston, Savannah, and Atlanta spent summers in Asheville specifically because the mountain air was tolerable when their home cities were not. The Grove Park Inn was built in part to capitalize on this need. The Biltmore Estate sits here, and not by accident.

That same advantage is still available and no longer requires a private fortune. On a July afternoon when Atlanta is logging its 60th day above 90 degrees, Asheville is having a perfectly pleasant 83-degree day with a thunderstorm in the afternoon and a 65-degree evening to follow.

The Asheville Chamber of Commerce has documented just 863 cooling degree days per year, compared to 4,195 heating degree days. In plain terms: you will always spend more on heat than on air conditioning. This is not something you can say in Charlotte, Atlanta, Raleigh, or most of the Southeast.

For the increasing number of people relocating from hotter climates, whether that's Phoenix, Dallas, or the inland valleys of California, Asheville's summers are not merely pleasant. They feel like being let out of something.

A Fall That Needs No Marketing (Unfortunately)

Every destination claims to have beautiful fall foliage. Asheville actually has it, and the reason is structural. The region's varied elevations and diverse tree species create one of the longest and most dramatic fall color seasons in North America, stretching from late September all the way into early November. This is either a six-week natural wonder or a six-week hostage situation, depending entirely on whether you have anywhere to be.

The show starts at the highest elevations in late September, above 6,000 feet, at places like Mount Mitchell and Graveyard Fields on the Blue Ridge Parkway. By early October it moves down to the 5,000-foot range, reaching Grandfather Mountain and the ridges around Beech Mountain. The second and third weeks of October bring color to the 3,000 to 4,000-foot zone, which includes long stretches of the Parkway itself. By late October and into November, the valleys and city streets are painted in golds and ambers. Sugar maples go scarlet. Red oaks turn burgundy. Sourwoods blaze crimson. It looks retouched in photographs and somehow even better in person.

What the photographs don't capture, and what the tourism brochures are careful not to mention, is what happens to every road, parking lot, overlook, and grocery store within forty miles of Asheville during this six-week period. You are no longer a resident of a mid-sized mountain city. You are an extra in a very slow movie that everyone else is filming from their car window.

The Blue Ridge Parkway on a Saturday in mid-October is not a drive. It is a procession. A pilgrimage. A rolling meditation on patience conducted at eleven miles per hour by people from Ohio and Florida who have never seen a deciduous tree change color and are processing the experience in real time. They will stop. Not at designated overlooks, though they'll stop at those too. They will stop anywhere. In the middle of the road, with no warning, because a particular sugar maple on a particular ridgeline has caught the light in a way that demands documentation. You will be behind them. You will have been behind them for twenty minutes already.

The Parkway is a two-lane road with no passing lanes, no traffic signals, and a speed limit of 45 that is treated as a suggestion. There are 469 miles of it, and during peak color season roughly a third of that mileage becomes a single-file convoy of rental cars driven by people who, to be entirely fair, are witnessing something genuinely extraordinary and simply cannot help themselves. You understand this. You even sympathize. This does not help you get to the hardware store.

Asheville proper, at around 2,200 feet, typically sees its own peak color in the last week of October. By this point, leaf-peeping season has been underway for three weeks, and the city has had time to develop a particular collective expression that blends civic pride with mild exhaustion. Locals learn to run their weekend errands on Tuesday mornings. They find the secondary overlooks, the ones without signs and without bus parking. They go to the Parkway at dawn, when the light is extraordinary and the only other people there are photographers with tripods who have made the same calculation.

The foliage itself is blameless in all of this. It is, without qualification, one of the great natural spectacles in the eastern United States. The mountains here run in long ridges, and when the trees along those ridges turn, you're looking at hillsides that stretch for miles in every direction. You are not visiting a park with some nice trees. You are inside a landscape in the middle of something extraordinary. On a clear October morning, driving south on the Parkway with the valleys below you and the ridgelines above lit up in every shade between gold and scarlet, it is impossible to be grumpy about it. You have just agreed to be grumpy about getting there, which is a fair trade.

Winter: The Goldilocks Proposition

Asheville's winters are cold enough to feel like winter. They are rarely cold enough to make you miserable.

The 30-year average for annual snowfall is about 9.9 inches, with some years coming in closer to 12 when you account for recent variability. January is the snowiest month, averaging 4.1 inches. February adds 2.2, March about 1.9, and December a modest 0.9. The average winter temperature is around 45 degrees, which is not Arctic.

What this means practically is that most years bring one decent snowfall, maybe a couple of dustings, and enough cold nights to justify a fireplace. You get the season without the grind. You do not have to shovel your driveway repeatedly for four months. You do not have to own a snow blower. You do not have to budget for salt and sand and the particular depression that comes from staring at gray slush in April.

What Asheville snow does bring, reliably, is that thing that happens when a place not built for snow gets a few inches. Schools close. The city quiets. People sled down steep neighborhood streets on whatever they can find. Restaurants close early or open late. There's a collective permission to stay inside, make soup, and not feel guilty about it. That lasts a day or two. Then it melts, and life resumes.

The school closure question deserves its own paragraph, because it is the source of considerable confusion among transplants from places that actually get winter. You will look out your downtown window on a snow day morning. You will see a perfectly clear, sunny, 45-degree day. The main roads will be dry. The sky will be a flawless winter blue. You will check your phone and discover that Buncombe County Schools and Asheville City Schools are closed, and you will experience a moment of genuine bewilderment.

Here is the explanation. Buncombe County is not a small city surrounded by flat suburbs. It is a geographically enormous county that includes river valleys, downtown streets, and steep north-facing mountain hollows where the sun does not reach until well into the morning and where the overnight temperature dropped to 24 degrees on roads that had no salt on them because the county runs on a budget. The school district operates large, heavy, rear-wheel-drive buses that must navigate all of it. Your downtown street, which is dry and pleasant, is not the constraint. The constraint is a shaded ridge road in the Reems Creek valley that is a solid sheet of black ice from the guardrail to the ditch, with a 20-degree gradient and a drop-off on one side that no school bus driver should be asked to negotiate with a load of children.

This is not a failure of nerve. It is an application of physics. A fully loaded school bus on black ice on a steep mountain grade does not stop. It does not slow down. It continues in whatever direction gravity and momentum have jointly decided, and no amount of braking changes this outcome in a meaningful way. The county transportation department knows which roads are problematic. They also know they cannot send half the buses and not the other half, because the children on the inaccessible routes also have parents, and those parents have opinions.

The transplants from Ohio and Minnesota who post on local Facebook groups every snow day about how back home we went to school in a blizzard are, on their own terms, not wrong. Schools in Cleveland do operate in conditions that would shut Asheville down for a week. What those transplants have not fully processed is that Cleveland is flat. Cleveland has a plowing fleet calibrated to its actual winters. Cleveland does not have bus routes that climb 800 feet in two miles on a road that a county truck has never salted in living memory because it only gets like this twice a year and the salt budget ran out in January. The physics do not care where you grew up. In Asheville, you are not subject to the weather at the airport. You are subject to the microclimate of the most treacherous road on the most vulnerable bus route in the county. That road closes school for everyone.

The variability is genuine and worth knowing about. Some winters bring almost nothing. In 2023 and 2024, Asheville recorded zero measurable snowfall. In other years, the mountains remind you where you live. In 2010, the city received 39.6 inches for the season. In January 2022, a single storm dropped 10.4 inches at the airport, exceeding the entire typical winter season in one event. The all-time seasonal record, set in 1969, is 49.5 inches.

You don't plan around Asheville snow. You celebrate it when it arrives and carry on when it doesn't. This is, arguably, the correct relationship to have with winter.

The Gardener's Reckoning

If you're the kind of person who moves somewhere and immediately starts thinking about what you can grow,

Asheville has both gifts and challenges waiting for you. Based on data from NC State University, the average last spring freeze at the Asheville Airport station occurs around April 20, and the first fall freeze arrives around October 17. Downtown Asheville, slightly lower in elevation and more sheltered by surrounding terrain, shows a last freeze around April 11 and first freeze around October 25. This gives the city a growing season of roughly 180 days, which is meaningful but shorter than Charlotte's, where the last frost averages April 1 and the first fall freeze arrives around November 5.

Asheville sits in USDA Hardiness Zone 7a, where winter lows range from 0 to 10 degrees Fahrenheit. Experienced local nurseries suggest planting for Zone 6 anyway, to account for the mountain microclimates, the cold-air drainage that settles in valleys overnight, and the exposed ridgelines where frost lingers past calendar expectations. The Buncombe County Extension office advises waiting until around Mother's Day to plant tender plants like tomatoes, peppers, and petunias, even when a warm April has made everything feel ready.

The real challenge for Asheville gardeners isn't cold. It's the volatility of spring. March can deliver a 70-degree Thursday followed by a 30-degree Saturday. A warm spell in early April encourages fruit trees to blossom, and then a late freeze cuts them back. South-facing slopes warm quickly while shaded hollows stay cold and damp through May. You learn to read the terrain, not just the forecast. The gardeners who thrive here are the ones who've made peace with the calendar, and found they enjoy the extra negotiation.

The Stories That Shaped the Relationship

Every place has its weather legends, the storms that become part of shared memory, the events people refer to when they want to understand where they live. Asheville has several, and they reveal something essential about what it means to live in a mountain landscape that channels enormous amounts of water.

The first of these events happened in July 1916, when two back-to-back hurricanes, one from the Gulf of Mexico and one from the Atlantic, arrived within days of each other. The result was more than 26 inches of rain falling on Western North Carolina in a single week.

The French Broad River crested at roughly 21 feet, or about 17 feet above flood stage. The floodwaters spread nearly a mile wide through Asheville. Biltmore Village was devastated. The railroad infrastructure connecting the region to the outside world was shattered, with 30 miles of track between Old Fort and Asheville either washed away or buried under landslides. Chimney Rock Village was effectively erased by boulders and racing water. At least 25 people died in Western North Carolina alone. For more than a century afterward, 1916 was the benchmark. Whenever the rivers rose, people asked how it compared. The flood shaped infrastructure decisions, building codes, and a quiet cultural wariness about the rivers that run through these mountain valleys.

The second defining event was the Blizzard of 1993. On March 12 and 13 of that year, a storm classified as Category 5 on the national scale made its way up the eastern seaboard and dropped 18 inches of snow on the Asheville airport in 48 hours, something that had never happened before and hasn't happened since. Mount Mitchell recorded 50-inch snowdrifts. Wind gusts reached hurricane force. The storm produced 60,000 lightning strikes across the Southeast, a meteorological combination so unusual that many people who lived through it still struggle to explain it to people who weren't here. It thundered while it snowed.

For two days. This is not a normal thing.

Before any of that happened, however, Asheville experienced something equally remarkable: the bread-and-milk run. In Asheville, a forecast for significant snow triggers a collective behavioral response that can only be described as a dry run for the end of civilization. The grocery stores empty. Not the exotic items. The basics. Every loaf of bread in Buncombe County disappears within hours of the first weather alert. The milk cases go next. Then the eggs. Then, somewhat mysteriously, the batteries. There is no rational explanation for why a two-day snowstorm requires eleven gallons of milk per household, but the data is clear.

The Ingles on Merrimon Avenue in the days before the Blizzard of '93 was, by all surviving accounts, a scene. The parking lot alone required a level of automotive optimism that bordered on the delusional. Inside, the checkout lines stretched to the back of the store. People who had not spoken to their neighbors in years found themselves united in solemn communion over the last remaining package of hamburger buns. There was no panic, exactly. It was more organized than panic. It was the calm, purposeful urgency of people who had been told by their television that something historic was coming and had decided, individually and collectively, that they would face it with enough Wonder Bread to last a month.

Then the storm arrived, and it turned out the television had undersold it.

Eighteen inches of snow fell on the Asheville airport. That is the official figure, measured in a flat, open location designed for accurate measurement. In the neighborhoods, particularly the ones with any elevation or exposure, the numbers were different. Drifts against houses. Cars buried to the door handles. Roads that didn't just close but disappeared, their existence temporarily theoretical. Mount

Mitchell, forty-some miles northeast, recorded fourteen-foot accumulations in places with fifty-inch drifts. The Army was eventually deployed to reach stranded residents in outlying communities. Emergency dispatchers worked by lantern light because the power was out and the temperature was dropping. Water had to be trucked in from other parts of the Carolinas.

Meanwhile, a cohort of UNC Asheville students who had been packed and mentally departed for spring break woke up to two and a half feet of snow outside their dormitory windows. Spring break was not happening. They were not going to the beach. They were going to be exactly here, in the mountains, watching it snow, for however long it took the state to dig out. The looks on their faces have not been described in surviving documents, but one can imagine.

What happened next is the part that people who lived through the '93 blizzard talk about at parties thirty years later. They were snowbound, most of them, for somewhere between two and five days. The power was out. The phones, in the pre-cell era, worked intermittently at best. The roads were impassable. And so people did what people do when modern infrastructure temporarily stops working: they talked to their neighbors. They pooled food. They sat around fireplaces. They walked to check on each other in snowdrifts that came to their knees. The city that had emptied Ingles of its bread in anticipation of catastrophe discovered that the actual catastrophe was, once you got past the cold soup and the lack of television, somewhat companionable.

The stories from the Blizzard of '93 have a specific texture. They're not just survival narratives. They're neighborhood stories, the kind where people find out who their neighbors actually are. They end, almost universally, with the roads clearing and someone saying, unprompted, that it was actually kind of nice. Then catching themselves and immediately clarifying that they would not want to do it again. Both things are true. The storm was genuinely terrible and genuinely formative, and the people who were here carry it with them the way you carry any experience that tested you and found you mostly adequate. If you move to Asheville and eventually mention to a long-timer that you were somewhere else in March of 1993, they will look at you with something between sympathy and mild pity. You missed it. You will hear about it for as long as you live here, and honestly, fair enough.

Helene: The Event That Reframed Everything

And then there is Hurricane Helene.

On September 27, 2024, the remnants of Hurricane Helene reached Western North Carolina. The Asheville airport recorded nearly 14 inches of rainfall in a three-day period. The region had already received heavy rain in the days prior, saturating the soil so thoroughly that the ground could absorb almost nothing. Every drop that fell ran directly into the rivers.

The French Broad River at Asheville crested more than a foot and a half above the 1916 record, the one that had stood as the benchmark for over a century. The Swannanoa River at Biltmore crested at 26.1 feet, more than five feet above its previous record. More than 2,000 landslides were documented across the region. Entire sections of Interstate 40 through the Pigeon River Gorge eroded or collapsed into the river below. The Blue Ridge Parkway sustained $1.7 billion in damage. Biltmore Village and the River Arts District, both low-lying and close to the rivers, were inundated. All roads in Western North Carolina were closed to non-emergency travel.

The city lost power, water service, and cell connectivity simultaneously. That sentence is doing a lot of quiet work, and it deserves to be unpacked.

The municipal water system for Asheville depends on infrastructure that lives in river valleys. When those valleys flooded, that infrastructure was damaged, contaminated, or simply gone. The taps stopped working. Not briefly. The city's water system would not be fully restored for weeks, and in some areas considerably longer. In the immediate aftermath, residents were advised not to use municipal water for any purpose, including brushing teeth. This is a city of roughly 95,000 people. It had no water.

The National Guard arrived. Uniformed soldiers in military vehicles established water distribution points across the city and county, where residents could collect potable water in whatever containers they owned. Jugs. Pots. Five-gallon buckets. Coolers with the ice long since melted. Distribution sites included the parking lot at UNC Asheville, the Enka-Candler area, Woodfin, and a rotating set of locations that the city communicated through whatever channels still worked. Cell service was down for large portions of the county for days. People learned where the water was the way people learn things when the internet doesn't work: from whoever they could find who knew.

Think about what no water means in daily terms. You cannot flush a toilet. You cannot wash a wound. You cannot cook food that requires boiling, rinse the mud off your hands after helping dig out a neighbor's car, or fill a glass for a child who is asking for water in the tone of voice that children use when they are not sure if things are going to be okay. Asheville in the days after Helene was a city that had been profiled in food magazines for its nationally recognized culinary identity, a place whose coffee shops had waitlists and whose restaurants had James Beard nominations. It was also, simultaneously, a city where residents stood in line with empty milk jugs waiting for a National

Guard truck. Both things were true at the same time. Holding that image matters. The mountain idyll and the military water distribution point exist in the same zip code.

Power was out across large swaths of the city and county for nearly a week in some areas, longer in others. No power means no refrigeration, which means the food on hand has a clock on it. It means no light after dark. It means no electric heat as the late-September nights turned cool. When cell service began returning, it returned partially and unpredictably. Knowing whether a family member in a different part of the county was safe required either going there or finding someone who had. Many people did both.

This is the context in which community cohesion was not a nice idea but a practical requirement. The people who stayed after Helene helped each other not only as an expression of values, though it was that too, but because the alternative was simply worse. Neighbors with generators ran extension cords to neighbors without. People with private wells shared water with people whose municipal taps had stopped working. Mutual aid networks formed in days because the city's formal support infrastructure was itself overwhelmed or damaged. People with chainsaws cleared roads before any municipal equipment could get there. The Asheville Recovers initiative brought thousands of volunteers into the hardest-hit areas. The community cohesion that people had moved to Asheville to find was tested in the hardest possible way and, mostly, held. Asheville is a place that people love deeply, and places that people love deeply ask something in return. The mountains are not a retreat from the world's difficulty. They are a specific version of it, with specific compensations.

The recovery has been long and in some places is still very much in progress. To understand what happened to Interstate 40, it helps to know what the Pigeon River Gorge is: a four-mile slot canyon cut into the mountains at the Tennessee border, where the river runs fast and cold through walls of exposed rock. I-40 was threaded through it because there was no other reasonable route between Asheville and Knoxville, built on whatever ledge could be blasted into shape alongside the river. More than 26,000 vehicles a day moved through that corridor. For decades, it held.

When Helene's rainfall hit the Pigeon River watershed, the gorge became a funnel inside a funnel. The river rose not in hours but in minutes, carrying trees, boulders, and entire sections of mountainside. In more than ten locations across those four miles, the eastbound lanes of I-40 simply ceased to exist. They did not wash out the way a road washes out in flat country. In the gorge, sections of highway fell into the river. The roadbed, the fill, the embankment behind it: gone, replaced by a fifty-foot cliff of raw mountain above fast water. The Pigeon River, which spent the Jurassic period carving this canyon long before any human road existed, took back a portion of the gorge it had made and appeared entirely unbothered by the transaction.

For five months, Interstate 40 at the Tennessee line was closed completely. There was an alternate route, of course. Back in Chapter 2, this book cheerfully mentioned that locals keep the I-26 north to I-81 south corridor in their back pocket as a workaround when I-40 gets ugly. What Chapter 2 did not fully convey is what keeping it in your back pocket means when it becomes your only option for five months. The detour adds roughly an hour and a half to the drive to Knoxville, threads through Wytheville, Virginia, and turns what used to be a 90-minute commute corridor into a logistical grudge match. Businesses recalculated freight costs. Trucks rerouted. People absorbed the reality that their primary connection west was not coming back quickly, and that the backup plan they had been quietly proud of was, in daily practice, deeply annoying. I-40 partially reopened in March 2025, which is when the isolation became visible.

If you drive that corridor today, you enter the gorge and the road narrows to a single lane in each direction, divided by a nine-inch concrete curb anchored into the asphalt. On your left, the rock wall of the gorge. On your right, beyond that low curb, the Pigeon River runs where the other lane used to be. Not metaphorically. The river is there, in the road's former footprint, below a raw cliff face where the eastbound lanes fell in. The speed limit is 35 miles an hour. You slow down not because the sign tells you to but because the geometry of the place makes speed feel inappropriate. Full reconstruction is not expected until late 2028. Many workers left the area after the storm. Some businesses chose not to reopen. More than $3 billion from the American Relief Act of 2024 has been allocated for North Carolina recovery programs, and the work continues at pace.

North Carolina's official storm-related death count reached 107 confirmed fatalities, with 42 of those in Buncombe County. Across all affected states, the total exceeded 250, making Helene the deadliest hurricane to strike the continental United States since Katrina in 2005. It matters in any honest conversation about Asheville's climate because it interrupted a story that had been building for years: Asheville as climate haven, a place people fled to from fire-prone Western states and hurricane-battered coastlines, drawn by cooler temperatures, mountain elevation, and a reputation for missing the worst of whatever the atmosphere was doing.

What Helene revealed was something the mountains have always known but that promotional materials had glossed over: the same geography that keeps Asheville cool, the steep ridges, the narrow valleys, the dense river networks, is the same geography that turns extreme rainfall into catastrophic, concentrated flooding. The mountains funnel water. The valleys contain it. When enough water falls fast enough, there is nowhere for it to go except through the places where people live. Asheville still has cooler summers, less drought risk, and no coastal storm surge exposure. Those advantages are real. They simply don't come with a guarantee.

What the River Knows

The French Broad River is one of the oldest rivers in the world. Geologists estimate its age at somewhere between 300 and 340 million years, which predates the Atlantic Ocean and most of the mountain range it currently runs through. The mountains rose up around it. The river simply continued flowing north, as it had been doing, because it was there first and saw no reason to change course on account of some new geology. This is worth keeping in mind when you are standing in the River Arts District, or Biltmore Village, or Oakley, looking at the river and thinking about where you might like to open a business or buy a house.

The French Broad and the Swannanoa, which joins it from the east just below downtown, are not decorative features. They are the primary drainage systems for an enormous mountain watershed. Every stream, creek, and tributary from the surrounding ridges eventually finds one of these two rivers. In normal times this makes them scenic and recreational and beloved. On summer evenings you can watch people float them on inner tubes, which is a perfectly pleasant way to spend an afternoon. The river is, in those moments, entirely convincing as a benign amenity.

The river has also, on multiple occasions in recorded history, demonstrated what it actually is: a very large, very fast, very indifferent hydraulic system that does not recognize municipal zoning ordinances, FEMA flood maps, or the considerable financial investment represented by a trendy coffee shop built twelve feet from the bank. In 1916 it spread nearly a mile wide through Asheville. In 2024, it exceeded that record by more than a foot and a half at its Asheville gauge, and the Swannanoa added 26 feet of its own. The river arts district is called the River Arts District because it is on the river. That is the whole situation, right there, in four words.

This is not a criticism of anyone who lives or works near these rivers. The land along them is beautiful, reasonably flat in a city that otherwise is not, and historically significant. It is also land that a 300-million-year-old river has been rearranging on its own schedule since before trees existed. The real estate industry, to its credit, is generally required to disclose flood zone status. What it cannot fully disclose is the specific combination of saturated soil plus remnant tropical circulation plus ten inches of rain in twenty-four hours that turns a property's flood zone from a legal category into a physical reality.

After Helene, the city began updating its flood plain maps, which had been drawn on historical data that September 2024 rendered incomplete. This is the correct response. It is also necessarily backward-looking. The maps will reflect what happened; they cannot fully anticipate what the river will decide to do next, in a climate that produces more intense storms from a warmer Gulf. The grumpy lesson is that you cannot out-legislate a mountain's hydrology. You can map it, respect it, and build with it in mind. You cannot make the watershed stop draining into the river. People have been learning this in Asheville since at least 1791, when the earliest written records document flooding along the Swannanoa. They learned it again in 1901, 1916, 2004, and 2024. The lesson has excellent retention. It does not stay learned.

If you are buying property near the French Broad or the Swannanoa, or near any of their tributary creeks, consult the current FEMA flood maps and the City of Asheville's post-Helene mapping updates. Then ask your future neighbors what the water looked like in September 2024. Then make your own decision, with eyes open. The river will not be offended either way. It has been here for 300 million years and is in no particular hurry.

The Climate Haven Question, Revisited

Before Helene, Asheville appeared on multiple lists of America's best climate refuges for the era of climate change. The city had adopted a Municipal Climate Action Plan setting goals for renewable energy, reduced emissions, and more sustainable infrastructure. Its combination of temperate weather, high elevation, and inland location made it an easy recommendation. After Helene, the conversation got more complicated, as it should.

North Carolina's state climatologist has noted that the state remains susceptible to severe rainfall and flooding from tropical systems, and that the mechanism is getting worse. Warmer oceans fuel more intense storms. A warmer atmosphere holds more water vapor, which means heavier rainfall when storms arrive. The mountains can't change their shape in response to this; they'll continue to funnel whatever water falls into the valleys below. Climate change has also given Asheville an additional 17 warm spring days compared to 1970, with more pronounced swings between warm spells and late freezes. This is hard on orchards, on early-blooming natives, and on farmers who've built businesses around a particular growing calendar.

The fundamentals, though, remain. Asheville averages 97 clear days per year. Annual rainfall is 45.57 inches, reasonably distributed across the seasons. The elevation-driven temperature advantage, roughly 7 to 10 degrees cooler than cities two hours away at lower elevations, isn't going away as the climate warms. If anything, that advantage becomes more valuable as baselines shift upward. For people weighing climate factors when choosing where to live, Asheville remains one of the more compelling options in the eastern United States. It's simply not a place where you can stop paying attention.

Microclimates: When Your Neighborhood Is Its Own Weather

One of the more humbling aspects of Asheville's climate for new arrivals is discovering that the weather forecast is an approximation. A useful approximation, but still an approximation. The forecast is for the airport. Your neighborhood may be having a different conversation.

The mountain terrain creates microclimates that vary dramatically over short distances. A south-facing slope in West Asheville warms faster in spring and stays warmer longer into fall than a shaded north-facing ridge on the other side of the same hill. Cold air drains downhill on still nights, which means the lowest-lying neighborhoods and valleys tend to be colder overnight than locations partway up the slopes. Downtown Asheville, surrounded by buildings that retain heat, runs warmer than the suburban neighborhoods outside the urban core.

The River Arts District and the neighborhoods along the French Broad and Swannanoa sit at the lowest elevations in the city, which makes them the warmest in summer and among the most frost-prone in spring and fall. They're also, as 2024 demonstrated with blunt clarity, the most flood-exposed. North Asheville climbs toward the ridges beyond Weaverville, runs cooler, and tends to get more snow when winter weather arrives. South Asheville, around Biltmore Forest and Arden, sits lower and benefits from longer growing seasons. Oakley, in the Swannanoa valley just east of downtown, sees flooding risk sooner than neighborhoods at higher elevation when the rivers rise.

The elevation gradient extends well beyond city limits. Brevard, about 30 miles southwest, sits in a bowl that captures moisture and averages over 70 inches of rain per year. Mount Mitchell, at 6,684 feet the highest peak east of the Mississippi River, can receive snow in any month of the year and averages summer temperatures in the mid-50s. You can be standing in warm October sunshine in Asheville and drive 45 minutes to find early winter on the summit.

For residents, learning the microclimates becomes part of local knowledge accumulated over time. You learn which roads ice first when temperatures drop, which hollows fill with fog on still mornings, and why the forecast for 58 degrees might mean 62 on your south-facing porch and 54 on the shaded side of the same house. For people who love weather, this is one of the more genuinely engaging aspects of daily life here. A kind of ongoing environmental literacy that you develop without really trying.

Rain: What 45 Inches Actually Means

Asheville averages 45.57 inches of rain per year, distributed across the seasons without a pronounced dry season. This matters because Asheville doesn't experience the summer drought that affects much of the South. The forests and rivers stay relatively full even in dry years, which is why the surrounding landscape looks the way it does. May and July tend to be the wettest months, driven by convective afternoon thunderstorms that build over the ridges, roll through quickly, and leave the air clean and cool behind them. October and November are the driest months, which is fortunate for leaf-peeping purposes. Experienced hikers time their summit attempts for the morning and plan to be below tree line before 2 p.m., which is about when the afternoon buildups start getting serious.

The Case for Weather That Talks Back

There is a version of climate that asks nothing of you. A place where every day is 72 and sunny, where the temperature varies by about 15 degrees across the year, where rain arrives politely at predictable intervals and doesn't overstay. Some people find this appealing. There are entire cities built on the promise of it. Asheville offers something different. It offers weather with a personality, and that personality is not always agreeable.

You get an October that makes you stop what you're doing and look up at the trees. You get a February morning with three inches of snow on everything and nothing to do but make coffee and sit by the window. You get a July afternoon thunderstorm that clears the air so thoroughly that the evening smells like the world just started. You get a March that can't decide what year it thinks it is, cycling through what feels like several seasons in a single week.

The climate here is not a backdrop. It participates. It shapes the agricultural calendar, the outdoor recreation options, the restaurant menus, the character of different neighborhoods, the stories that people tell at parties. It gives longtime residents a shared vocabulary. Ask someone who's been here a decade about the Blizzard of '93 and they'll either tell you where they were, or ask their parents. Ask about Helene and the room gets quiet in a specific way that you'll understand if you were here.

People who've moved here from flat, hot, climate-controlled cities often describe a gradual shift in how they relate to being outside. They start tracking the weather not to manage it but because they're interested. They learn the forecast the way you learn a new person's habits. They stop treating rain as an inconvenience and start treating it as information. That shift isn't for everyone. Some people want their weather solved. If that describes you, Asheville will try your patience roughly nine months of the year. But for people who find it appealing, the climate here is, in the most genuine sense of the word, a feature.

Practical Things to Know Before You Arrive

The roads are not built for ice. When temperatures drop and moisture is present, the steep hills throughout the city become problematic quickly. Most long-term residents have all-wheel or four-wheel drive, and even those vehicles require respect on a steep Asheville hill that's glazed over at 6 a.m. Mountain topography has limits that sand trucks can't entirely overcome. If you're looking at a house on a steep road, ask the neighbors what winter mornings are like. They will tell you the truth.

Fall is genuinely crowded. October in Asheville is peak tourism season, and the Blue Ridge Parkway on a weekend in mid-October is not a peaceful drive. It's a very slow drive with excellent scenery and out-of-state license plates from everywhere. If you're a resident rather than a visitor, you learn to go early in the morning or on weekdays, or to find the secondary overlooks that the tour buses don't stop at. The foliage doesn't care either way. It's spectacular regardless of the traffic.

Tropical storm season requires awareness. This is a mountain city that has, twice in its recorded history, experienced catastrophic flooding from the remnants of Gulf and Atlantic storms. Tropical activity peaks from late August through mid-October. When a major storm makes landfall somewhere on the Gulf Coast or the Atlantic, monitoring what its inland track means for western North Carolina is now a reasonable part of seasonal life. This doesn't mean living in fear. It means having a plan, knowing your flood zone status, and paying attention to the French Broad and Swannanoa river gauges when serious rain is in the forecast.

The view from almost anywhere is better than you expect. This sounds like tourism copy, but it's a practical point. Living at elevation means that the visual backdrop of daily life in Asheville includes mountains in nearly every direction. You stop noticing after a while, which is one of the stranger psychological adaptations to living somewhere beautiful. But visitors notice it immediately, and occasionally it catches you off guard too, usually in the morning or in that particular fall light, and you remember where you are and feel, briefly, like someone who made a very good decision.

What the Climate Gives You That You Didn't Know to Ask For

Before moving to Asheville, most people focus on the obvious climate benefits. Cooler summers. Pretty falls. Manageable winters. All of that is real. What they don't anticipate is how it changes how you live. It changes where you spend time and who you spend it with. It changes your relationship to the city itself, because you're experiencing more of it at street level and less of it through a windshield or an air conditioner. The weather here extends an open invitation for most of the year, which is not something that most American cities can honestly claim.

The honest case for Asheville's climate is not that it's perfect or safe or stable. It's that it's four-seasoned, genuinely livable, and worth the engagement it requires. October's beauty and September 2024's destruction came from the same mountains, by the same mechanism. Neither cancels the other out. Living here means holding both.

Don't plant your tomatoes before Mother's Day. Keep an eye on the rivers when the rain comes hard. Show up for October like it's the best thing all year, because most years it is.

Just don't say nobody warned you about March.

CHAPTER SIX

DON'T MOVE HERE IF YOU'RE PLANNING TO GET OLD OR SICK

Let's get this mythology out of the way immediately. The story goes that Asheville is a charming little mountain town with a charming little mountain hospital, and if something truly serious happens to you, your best option involves a helicopter and a very clear view of the Blue Ridge Parkway from about 3,000 feet. People repeat this story at dinner parties in Atlanta and Charlotte and Sarasota when someone mentions they're thinking about moving to Asheville. It gets told with the kind of confident authority that usually indicates the speaker has not done any actual research. You should absolutely not move here, and if medical mythology is your reason, you should find a better one.

The mythology is wrong. Asheville anchors one of the most developed healthcare ecosystems in the rural Southeast, with a Level I trauma center, more than a thousand physicians practicing across dozens of specialties, an active medical education pipeline, a fast-expanding competitive landscape, and a surrounding network of regional hospitals that would be the envy of many cities twice its size. The infrastructure is here. The question, and it is a genuinely important one, is whether the largest player in that infrastructure is meeting its obligations, and what your options look like when it falls short.

Both of those questions have complicated answers. Let's start with the flagship. It has the most complicated answer of all, and I am going to need you to stay with me.

Mission Hospital: The Dominant Force

Mission Hospital sits at 509 Biltmore Avenue in the heart of Asheville, a ten-minute walk from the art galleries and craft breweries of downtown. It is, by any reasonable measure, the dominant medical institution in Western North Carolina. The hospital operates 837 staffed beds, approximately 90 adult ICU beds, and a Level III Neonatal Intensive Care Unit. In December 2025, Mission earned verification as an ACS Level I Trauma Center, upgrading from Level II — the only such designation in the 18-county Western North Carolina region. It runs a Comprehensive Stroke Center and is the home base for MAMA, the Mountain Area Medical Airlift, the region's emergency helicopter service. WebMD lists 79 specialties and 1,018 practicing physicians on its campus.

That Level I designation is not a marketing label. It means that for the most catastrophic medical emergencies — major car crash injuries, crush injuries, amputations, severe burns, spinal cord injuries, complex pelvic and thoracic fractures, and multiple simultaneous injuries requiring surgical specialists on call around the clock — Mission is the mandatory destination. No other hospital in the region has the staff, equipment, or certification to manage those at this level. When the helicopter lands, it lands here.

The same logic applies to cardiac emergencies. Mission operates an Advanced Cardiac Care center and is actively participating in national clinical trials, including a ground-breaking TAVR stroke-protection trial. For heart attacks, cardiac arrest, and complex cardiac surgery, Mission is the only local option. The nearest alternatives are Charlotte, about two hours away, and Greenville, South Carolina, roughly an hour to the south. You do not want to be making either drive during a cardiac event.

For stroke, Mission holds the American Heart Association's Get With The Guidelines Stroke Gold Plus award and has earned the Target: Stroke Honor Roll Elite Plus designation, meaning it has some of the fastest clot-busting and clot-removal response times in the country. Stroke treatment is brutally time-sensitive. The clinical shorthand is "time is brain," and it is accurate. Mission is where you need to be.

Mission also houses the only Level III NICU in the region, equipped to care for infants born before 32 weeks or under 3.3 pounds and any newborn with a critical illness. The Carolina Spine and Neurosurgery Center, affiliated with Mission, is the only comprehensive neurosurgical practice in Western North Carolina, covering brain aneurysms, cerebral tumors, hydrocephalus, arteriovenous malformations, and complex spinal surgery. And Mission is the only local provider of ECMO, extracorporeal membrane oxygenation, the last-resort life-support technology used when heart or lungs fail entirely. These are not services you shop around for. They are services that exist here and nowhere else within a two-hour radius.

Mission Health traces its roots to 1885, when women from the 'Little Flower Mission' made house calls to patients throughout the mountain counties. Over the following century it grew into a six-hospital system stretching across the western counties: the flagship in Asheville, Angel Medical Center in Franklin, Blue Ridge Regional Hospital in Spruce Pine, Highlands-Cashiers Hospital, McDowell Hospital in Marion, and Transylvania Regional Hospital in Brevard. It established seven Centers of Excellence in cancer, heart, neurosciences, orthopedics, trauma, women's health, and pediatrics through Mission Children's Hospital, the only dedicated children's hospital in the region.

For most of its existence, Mission was a well-regarded non-profit community hospital system that genuinely functioned as a community asset. Then, in 2019, everything changed.

I want to be clear about something before we go further. What follows is not rumor, not the grievances of disgruntled former employees, and not the exaggerations of people who prefer their medical care accompanied by crystals and essential oils. It is a documented, litigated, federally sanctioned, Attorney General-verified record of what happens when the largest for-profit hospital chain in the country buys a community hospital and runs it like a profit center. I am going to tell you all of it, because you deserve to know. The full picture is worth having.

The HCA Acquisition: What Happened Next

In February 2019, HCA Healthcare, the largest for-profit hospital chain in the United States, purchased Mission Health for $1.5 billion. The sale was conducted largely behind closed doors by Mission's own leadership, and the proceeds went to create the Dogwood Health Trust, a philanthropic foundation intended to address social determinants of health across the region. This is the part where a billion and a half dollars sounds like a very good deal, until you understand what a billion and a half dollars bought. At the time of the sale, then-CEO Dr. Ronald Paulus received approximately $4 million in total compensation in Mission's final year of independence before departing to a consulting role with HCA. Make of that what you will. Most people make quite a lot of it.

The Dogwood Health Trust deserves a paragraph of its own, because it is what the community received in exchange for its hospital system, and it is what many residents cite when they want to explain why they feel so thoroughly taken. A billion and a half dollars is a staggering sum by the standards of nonprofit philanthropy, and the Trust has distributed meaningful grants across the region for housing, food security, mental health, and broadband access. What it cannot do, by its very structure, is practice medicine. It cannot hire back the more than 200 physicians who left the system after the acquisition. It cannot reopen the neurology and urology departments that were gutted. It cannot compel a corporation whose 2023 net income was approximately $4.6 billion to staff its emergency department adequately. A new community garden funded by a Dogwood grant is a genuinely nice thing, but it will not stitch up your laceration or deliver an oxygen tank when a nurse, stretched across seven patients instead of four, misses a discharge detail. The community traded its only functioning Level I trauma center for a very large grant-making foundation. Whether that was a wise trade is a debate that will outlast this book.

North Carolina's Attorney General negotiated an Asset Purchase Agreement requiring HCA to maintain critical services, including emergency, trauma, and oncology care, at pre-acquisition levels through at least 2029. What followed was a cascade of complaints, lawsuits, federal sanctions, and community outrage that fundamentally reshaped how Western North Carolina talks about its healthcare.

The problems surfaced almost immediately. Nurses began reporting dangerous staffing shortages and filed 'Assignment Despite Objection' forms documenting unsafe patient loads. In September 2020, Mission nurses voted to join the National Nurses United union for the first time in the hospital's history, citing concerns over patient safety and staffing.

Stop here for a moment. I want to make sure this next part lands.

It is worth pausing on what an Assignment Despite Objection form actually represents. It is not a complaint. It is a legal document a nurse files to create a written record stating: I am taking this patient load because I have no choice, and I want it on record that I believe it is unsafe. Before HCA, Mission operated at 6.0 full-time equivalent staff per occupied bed. By 2021 that number had dropped to 3.7, while comparable North Carolina hospitals held steady at 5.1. The distance between 3.7 and 5.1 is the difference between a nurse managing four patients and a nurse managing seven. It is the difference between catching a deteriorating patient in the early warning signs and catching them in a crisis. Those ADO forms piled up across years of 12-hour shifts while ambulances sat idle outside the emergency department in 'wall times,' waiting for somewhere to put patients, and the cancer center quietly lost every medical oncologist on its staff. The forms documented the erosion in real time. Federal regulators eventually came to see the results in person.

That is what the ADO forms were. Now you know what they were. Keep that in mind for the rest of this section.

A Wake Forest University study documented the scale of the physician exodus. More than 200 doctors left Mission in the years following the acquisition — a loss the study describes as hundreds of departures that gutted key specialties. HCA closed or defunded less profitable service lines. Otolaryngology, urology, rheumatology, and significant portions of orthopedics and neurology were depleted or effectively eliminated. Most consequentially, essentially all of Mission's medical oncologists departed, leaving its marquee cancer center practically deserted. Mission's patient-care profits rebounded to almost $100 million by 2022, roughly 3.5 times pre-acquisition levels, driven primarily by those staff cuts. The math worked out beautifully, if you were not one of the patients. The community paid for that rebound in delayed care, depleted specialties, and a cancer center that functioned without an oncologist.

Lawsuits, Sanctions, and Angry Attorneys General

In December 2023, Attorney General Josh Stein sued HCA, alleging the company had breached the Asset Purchase Agreement by significantly degrading emergency department and oncology services. The lawsuit cited extremely long ER wait times, severe staffing shortages, treatment of patients in bays that were neither private nor sterile, and a cancer center that no longer employed a single medical oncologist on staff. The state had received more than 500 complaints about care at HCA facilities across western North Carolina.

Buncombe County filed its own federal complaint in September 2024, documenting a $3 million impact to county taxpayers caused by HCA's policy changes. The county alleged that HCA began requiring patients transferred from rural hospitals to first be routed through Mission's Emergency Department, a practice that inflated bills and overcrowded the ER. EMS crews reported dramatically increased 'wall times' waiting to hand off patients, meaning ambulances that should have been back in service were sitting idle outside the hospital.

The cities of Asheville and Brevard, along with Buncombe and Madison Counties, filed a consolidated federal antitrust lawsuit alleging that HCA's hospital system held a monopoly on healthcare in the region, creating an anti-competitive market that harmed access and affordability. That suit settled in August 2025, with Mission agreeing to a $1 million donation to a charity care fund and a promise to continue operating Transylvania Regional Hospital for an additional three years. HCA's 2023 net income was approximately \$4.6 billion, which means the settlement represented roughly four hours of corporate profit. To put that differently: HCA generated the cash to settle with the county, the cities, and its neighbors in approximately the same amount of time a patient might spend waiting in Mission's overcrowded emergency department. The symmetry is not lost on anyone who has done both. HCA's lawyers presumably have not had to do both.

The Federal Scorecard

If you want one number that tells you everything, here it is. Immediate Jeopardy is the harshest sanction CMS can levy against a healthcare facility. It means deficiencies are severe enough to endanger patients' lives. Even one Immediate Jeopardy finding is considered extraordinary for a major hospital.

Mission has received Immediate Jeopardy status four times since the HCA acquisition: in 2021, early 2024, October 2025, and January 2026. The January 2026 designation followed state inspectors documenting incidents including the deaths of two patients, with investigators finding that staff errors, communication breakdowns, and equipment failures had put patients' lives at risk. The January 2026 finding marked the third Immediate Jeopardy designation in less than two years.

Other HCA-owned facilities in the region have faced their own sanctions. Blue Ridge Regional Hospital in Spruce Pine received an Immediate Jeopardy citation in 2023, and Mission Hospital McDowell in Marion received one in 2021.

As of early March 2026, Mission's most recent Immediate Jeopardy status was lifted after CMS approved the hospital's Enhanced Plan of Correction. Nurses on the ground have consistently warned that such corrections are not sustained.

They have been right before. The hospital is currently operating at roughly three-quarters of its needed nursing staff, according to nurses who track the numbers closely.

The Community Fights Back

A coalition called Reclaim Healthcare WNC formed in 2024, bringing together physicians, nurses, elected officials, clergy, and community advocates to pressure HCA to improve conditions or relinquish ownership of Mission. The coalition's leadership includes State Senator Julie Mayfield and the mayors of Brevard and Highlands. Their goals are straightforward: hold HCA accountable and empower residents to be their own healthcare advocates.

The numbers on the coalition's website tell the story bluntly. Since HCA purchased Mission Health, more than 200 physicians and 600 nurses have left the system. In February 2026, coalition members urged CMS to investigate Mission's patient discharge practices, citing reports of patients being sent home without necessary equipment, including oxygen.

This is not a fringe movement of cranky locals. It is a broad, organized, professionally led effort that has attracted serious attention from state and federal regulators. The fact that it needs to exist is the problem. The fact that it does exist is, in its own way, reassuring.

You now know more about Mission Hospital than most people who live within ten minutes of it. That is either alarming or clarifying, depending on your disposition. I am going to choose to find it clarifying, and I would invite you to do the same — because the rest of this chapter is considerably more cheerful, and you have earned it.

The Competition Is Coming, and It Cannot Arrive Fast Enough

For decades, Mission operated as effectively the only major game in Buncombe County for serious medical care. That monopoly is cracking, and three competing hospital systems are actively pushing into the market. Understanding them is essential for anyone building a life here, and frankly for anyone looking for reasons not to.

AdventHealth is the most aggressive new entrant. The Florida-based nonprofit system already operates AdventHealth Hendersonville, a full-service hospital about 25 minutes south of Asheville on US-64. In November 2022, the North Carolina Department of Health and Human Services approved AdventHealth's Certificate of Need application to build a new community hospital on a 30-acre site in Weaverville, just north of Asheville off Interstate 26. The original approval covered 67 beds, with a labor and delivery unit, an emergency department, ICU beds, and surgical suites. A subsequent Certificate of Need for 26 additional beds brought the total approved to 93. AdventHealth has since applied for a further 129 beds, which would bring the planned facility to 222 beds and make it the region's second-largest hospital behind Mission.

HCA appealed the Certificate of Need decision and fought construction through multiple courts for more than three years. In December 2025, the North Carolina Supreme Court declined to hear HCA's final appeal, ending the legal battle and clearing the way for construction to begin. HCA's willingness to spend years in court fighting a competitor's right to build a hospital is at least philosophically consistent with everything else in this chapter.

UNC Health Pardee in Hendersonville is a nonprofit community hospital affiliated with the UNC Health Care System. It offers a Level II Trauma Center, comprehensive surgical services, ICU, rehabilitation, women's health, and maternity care. Pardee has been expanding its footprint, opening a new Brevard campus in March 2026, and operating multiple primary care locations in Arden, Mills River, and along the Hendersonville Road corridor heading into south Asheville. For residents of south Asheville and Henderson County, Pardee is often the most practical alternative to Mission for non-emergency care.

Novant Health, the Winston-Salem-based nonprofit, has built a presence in Western North Carolina through urgent care centers in Black Mountain and Asheville, an imaging center, and a surgical practice covering oncology, breast, colorectal, and endocrine surgery. Novant submitted a proposal to build a 26-bed cancer-focused hospital on a 24-acre site at 455 Long Shoals Road near Biltmore Park in south Asheville. In 2025, Novant announced plans to seek a Certificate of Need for 129 additional acute-care beds. The system has also committed $20 million over five years to develop rural primary care across the region.

Knowing these systems exist is useful. Knowing when to use which one is more useful. The practical map looks like this. For anything that requires Mission's Level I capabilities — trauma, cardiac emergencies, stroke, neurosurgery, ECMO, premature newborns — you go to Mission, full stop, because nothing else in the region can handle those. For everything else, the geography of where you live largely determines your best alternative. If you are in South Asheville, AdventHealth Hendersonville is your most instinctive non-emergency alternative, sitting about 25 minutes south on US-64 through Fletcher — the same road South Asheville residents are already on. Pardee in Hendersonville is nearby and serves the same general corridor. Once the Weaverville campus eventually opens, northside residents will have a closer option than they do today.

Novant is the one to watch for oncology and surgical specialties as its south Asheville footprint grows. The point is that a functional healthcare strategy for life in Asheville is not complicated, but it does require knowing that Mission is not your only choice for the vast majority of medical needs you will actually have.

The Wider Regional Network

Beyond the competition pressing into Asheville itself, the surrounding mountain counties have their own hospital infrastructure worth knowing.

Haywood Regional Medical Center in Clyde, about 30 minutes west on US-74, is a 154-bed facility affiliated with Duke LifePoint Healthcare. Founded in 1927, it offers behavioral health, cardiology, emergency medicine, general surgery, orthopedics, spine services, and women's care, along with 11 multi-specialty physician clinics and a fitness center on campus. It serves as the primary hospital for Haywood County and sees a significant volume of Asheville-area residents who live on the western side of town.

Harris Regional Hospital in Sylva, also a Duke LifePoint facility, operates 86 beds and serves the southwestern mountain counties with emergency, surgical, and women's services. Erlanger Western Carolina Hospital in Murphy, at the far western tip of the state, holds 191 licensed beds as part of the Chattanooga-based Erlanger Health System, though 120 of those are nursing home beds. The hospital controversially discontinued labor and delivery services in late 2020.

UNC Health Blue Ridge in Morganton, on the eastern edge of the mountain region, operates 184 beds as a nonprofit hospital serving Burke County. And the Charles George VA Medical Center on Tunnel Road in Asheville has served veterans since 1922, offering care across dozens of specialties to approximately 49,000 veterans in a 23-county service area across western North Carolina. If you are a veteran, the Charles George VA is a significant part of the healthcare equation here.

MAHEC: The Pipeline Worth Knowing

One of Asheville's most underappreciated healthcare assets is the Mountain Area Health Education Center, known everywhere as MAHEC. Founded in 1974, MAHEC is the largest Area Health Education Center in North Carolina, serving the state's 16 westernmost counties. It functions as a branch campus of UNC's schools of medicine, dentistry, pharmacy, and public health.

MAHEC runs family medicine and OB/GYN residency programs, trains the region's only board-certified maternal-fetal medicine specialists, and operates patient care clinics across the area. Its Center for Healthy Aging focuses specifically on geriatric care and wellness for older adults.

The practical effect of MAHEC's presence is that Asheville continuously produces and attracts new physicians in a way that smaller mountain communities simply cannot. It helps explain why the area has one of the highest concentrations of physicians per capita in the state for a city of its size, even accounting for the departures that followed HCA's acquisition. The pipeline keeps flowing.

Integrative Health: Not What You Might Expect

Asheville has cultivated a substantial bench of integrative and alternative health practitioners, and it would be misleading to treat this as a quirky footnote. For many people who specifically plan their retirements around having access to holistic healthcare options, this is a primary draw. The concentration of this kind of care here is genuinely unusual for a city of Asheville's size, and it did not happen by accident.

Asheville is also home to a substantial network of mental health practitioners, including therapists, psychologists, and psychiatry practices that work specifically with older adults navigating life transitions. The city has more licensed therapists per capita than most of its southeastern peers, a fact worth examining from two angles. The flattering interpretation is that it reflects an educated, self-aware population that values mental health care. The equally valid interpretation is that when you are managing a housing cost index of 113.3, watching your rent climb, and discovering that your pristine retirement destination features a flagship hospital under federal sanctions, professional psychological support stops being a luxury and starts being infrastructure. The therapists are here because the need is here. Either way, the resource exists, and in a city full of people who moved specifically to start the next chapter of their lives, that turns out to matter quite a bit.

None of this is the fringe. In Asheville, integrative health is part of the mainstream medical conversation, which means it comes with insurance billing practices, coordination with conventional providers, and the kind of clinical infrastructure that makes it actually usable as part of a healthcare plan rather than a supplement to one. If you are the kind of person who has spent years navigating the gap between what conventional medicine offers and what you actually want from your healthcare, Asheville is the first place many people describe as feeling like the gap has mostly closed.

All of which brings you to the next practical question, which every serious relocation candidate gets to eventually: where, exactly, are you going to live? This is not a trivial question in a city with as much geographic variation as Asheville, and it turns out to connect directly back to healthcare in ways that are worth understanding before you start browsing real estate listings. Your proximity to Mission, to Pardee, to AdventHealth, and to the urgent care options scattered across the metro varies considerably depending on which neighborhood or satellite community you land in. The medical map and the neighborhood map are the same map. Here is what the terrain actually looks like.

Where Retirees Actually End Up Living

Asheville's neighborhoods have distinct personalities, and the ones that tend to attract retirees are worth understanding before you start looking at real estate listings.

Biltmore Forest is an incorporated town within the Asheville metro, established in the 1920s adjacent to the Biltmore Estate. Its winding, canopied roads are lined with stately homes on generous lots, architecture ranging from Tudor and Georgian Revival to mid-century estates. The Biltmore Forest Country Club anchors the social scene with a Donald Ross-designed golf course. It sits ten minutes south of downtown and right along the Blue Ridge Parkway, which matters enormously for access to some of the most beautiful recreational driving and hiking in the eastern United States.

Kenilworth, tucked between downtown and Biltmore Village, was developed in the 1920s as its own self-contained village and retains a quiet charm that draws both medical professionals and retirees. Its location puts Mission Hospital within five minutes and downtown Asheville at the same distance. Kenilworth Lake offers a peaceful walking loop, and the neighborhood has no through traffic, which in a city of Asheville's increasing busyness is a genuine selling point.

Historic Montford, just north of downtown, is a designated Historic District of Victorian, Arts and Crafts, and Colonial Revival homes built primarily between 1890 and 1920. It is walkable to downtown restaurants and shops, hosts summer Shakespeare performances at the Hazel Robinson Amphitheatre, and retains the feeling of a small southern town from another era even as Asheville has grown around it. The housing stock is diverse enough that entry points exist well below what you would pay in Biltmore Forest.

South Asheville along the Hendersonville Road corridor is where many of the area's 55-plus communities cluster, with easy access to AdventHealth Hendersonville and Pardee, the Blue Ridge Parkway, and the Biltmore Park Town Square shopping district. Weaverville to the north and Black Mountain to the east offer small-town quiet with Asheville amenities a short drive away, and both are worth serious consideration for anyone who wants to feel like they actually live in a small mountain town rather than an increasingly busy mid-sized city.

West Asheville and East Asheville attract retirees less frequently, but they do attract them. West Asheville, centered on the Haywood Road corridor, skews younger and has the energy of a neighborhood still figuring itself out — good restaurants, strong arts presence, walkable pockets, and a general sense that someone nearby is probably in a band. Retirees who specifically want urban neighborhood character over residential quiet find it here. East Asheville, heading out toward Black Mountain along US-70, is quieter and more residential, and has one particular asset worth noting: it puts you close to the Charles George VA Medical Center on Tunnel Road, which for veterans is a meaningful geographic consideration.

The Retirement Communities You Will Wait For

Asheville and its surroundings support a network of continuing care retirement communities that people research and join waitlists for years in advance. This is not a soft market. The communities here are not the kind of institutional, beige-corridor places that give retirement living a bad name. They are set into the landscape in ways that remind you daily why you moved to the mountains.

Givens Estates on Sweeten Creek Road is the area's most established continuing care retirement community, and was ranked the number one retirement community in North Carolina by Newsweek for 2026. Sitting on a 215-acre campus, it houses approximately 800 residents across independent living cottages, duplexes, apartments, assisted living, and an 84-bed skilled nursing center. Affiliated with the United Methodist Church and accredited by CARF, monthly costs range from approximately $1,495 to $7,000 depending on the level of care. What you are buying at a community like Givens is not just housing. It is the guarantee that if your health needs change, you do not have to move again. The continuum of care on a single campus means you can start in an independent cottage and age in place through every subsequent level of need without uprooting your social world. Givens also operates Givens Gerber Park, a rental retirement community for adults 55-plus in urban south Asheville, and Givens Highland Farms in the small town of Black Mountain, which gives the organization a geographic footprint that covers most of the scenarios a new resident might be weighing.

Givens Communities also operates Givens Choice, a Continuing Care at Home membership program that represents a genuinely different way of thinking about the entire problem. Givens Choice is for people who want to age in their own homes but want the security net of a life plan community available if their needs escalate. Do not mistake the waitlists at communities like this for a polite queue at a country club. You are competing against an incoming wave of well-heeled retirees arriving with equity from homes in New Jersey, Illinois, and California, all reaching for the same finite number of spots. Securing a place in Asheville's senior care infrastructure — whether on a campus or in a home-based membership program — is a game that rewards people who plan ahead and penalizes people who wait.

Members of Givens Choice pay a one-time enrollment fee and a monthly fee that does not increase as their care needs change. They receive a dedicated Care Navigator who builds an ongoing relationship with them, coordinates services proactively rather than reactively, and connects them to the full range of Givens home care resources when the time comes. Three plan tiers offer different levels of coverage, from comprehensive to paired with an existing long-term care insurance policy. Benefits begin when a member needs help with just one activity of daily living, versus the two that most long-term care insurance policies require before they pay. That single-activity trigger is not a small distinction when you are the person who needs help.

The catch — and Givens Choice states it plainly, which is the right thing to do — is that half of people who apply after waiting too long fail the mandatory health screening. The program's logic is ruthlessly simple: the time to join is when you are healthy, not when you need it. It is a game of musical chairs played in slow motion over a decade, and the music stops at the exact moment you realize you should have picked a chair sooner. You are reading this now. The chair is right there. It would be a shame to still be thinking about it when the music stops.

Deerfield Episcopal Retirement Community on Hendersonville Road is a not-for-profit Life Care community offering independent living cottages and apartments, assisted living, and skilled nursing. Deerfield's partnership with MAHEC's Family Medicine Program means residents have a nurse practitioner and two physicians available on campus five mornings a week. That is not a minor convenience. For someone managing multiple chronic conditions, having a primary care provider who can walk across the courtyard to see you rather than requiring a car trip and a waiting room is a genuine quality-of-life difference. Deerfield's Aquatic Center, with a lap pool and a warm-water therapy pool, anchors an active wellness program that many residents describe as one of the primary reasons they chose the community.

Pisgah Valley Retirement Community in nearby Candler offers patio homes in the scenic Hominy Valley for residents 62 and older, with independent living, assisted living, and skilled nursing all on one campus. The Candler location puts residents about fifteen minutes west of downtown Asheville with a decidedly more rural character, which suits a certain kind of person very well. Brooks-Howell Home on Merrimon Avenue is a faith-based community in north Asheville originally established for United Methodist deaconesses and missionaries, now open to the broader community, and carries a resident satisfaction rating of 9.7 out of 10. Harmony at Reynolds Mountain offers independent living, assisted living, and memory care with long mountain views from a location in north Asheville that many residents describe as the best of both worlds: suburban quiet with a fifteen-minute drive to downtown.

Ardenwoods in Arden and Crowfields in south Asheville round out the primary options for those who want community living without a full continuing care commitment. Crowfields sits on 72 wooded acres with 192 units restricted to residents 55 and older, offering garden plots, a heated pool, and a clubhouse two minutes from the Blue Ridge Parkway. It is the kind of place where people move in their early sixties and stay for thirty years, which is the most honest endorsement any community can receive.

Once you have a sense of where you want to live and what kind of community structure appeals to you, the next question is unavoidable: what is all of this going to cost? That question has a complicated answer in Asheville, because the city rewards some financial situations and punishes others in ways that are not always obvious from the outside. The cost of living here is not outrageous, but it is not modest either, and understanding its specific contours matters considerably more than knowing the headline index number.

The Cost of Living Conversation

According to the C2ER Cost of Living Index compiled by the Asheville Area Chamber of Commerce using 2025 annual average data, Asheville's overall cost of living index sits at 106.8, meaning costs run about 6.8 percent above the national average. Housing drives most of that premium, registering at 113.3 on the index. Healthcare costs come in at 115.3, notably above the national average, while utilities at 95.6 and transportation at 92.7 actually run below it.

The median home price in the Asheville metro ranges roughly between $450,000 and $600,000 depending on timing and data source. A two-bedroom apartment rents for a median of about $1,703 per month. Monthly energy bills average around $196, which is considerably lower than you would pay in most northern cities and reflects both the mild climate and the area's relatively modest cooling load.

That utility number deserves a moment of attention. Most people moving from the Northeast or Midwest budget for heating costs and forget entirely to budget for the absence of them. Asheville sits at roughly 2,134 feet of elevation, which means summers are genuinely temperate by southern standards. Average July highs hover around 83 degrees. You will run your air conditioning, but you will not run it the way you would in Atlanta or Charlotte or Phoenix. The combination of mild summers and relatively short winters produces energy bills that come as a pleasant surprise to most transplants after the first full year.

Groceries track close to the national average. The city has a full complement of mainstream options including multiple Harris Teeter and Ingles locations, an Aldi, a Trader Joe's, and a Whole Foods, alongside the locally beloved French Broad Food Co-op and a robust farmers market scene. If you cook at home most of the time, which most retirees on fixed incomes tend to do, grocery costs here will not punish you.

Dining out is the variable that catches people. Asheville has developed a restaurant scene that punches well above its weight class, and the prices at the better establishments reflect that. You are not paying Manhattan prices, but you are also not paying Greenville, South Carolina, prices. A dinner for two at one of the James Beard-recognized establishments will run $150 to $200 without difficulty. The good news is that Asheville also has a full tier of excellent casual restaurants, taco spots, ramen shops, and neighborhood joints where two people eat well for $40. The city rewards people who learn to navigate its price tiers.

For retirees doing the math against their fixed income, the comparison to peer cities is instructive. Asheville's overall index of 106.8 is virtually identical to Chapel Hill at 106.6 but notably higher than Nashville at 98.5, Charleston at 96.3, Raleigh at 94.8, Atlanta at 94.7, and Greenville, South Carolina, at 90.6. You are paying a premium to be here, and that premium is real. But it is not San Francisco at 163.7 or Manhattan at 239.0. In the landscape of desirable mid-sized American cities with access to mountains and culture,

Asheville is expensive without being absurd.

The honest framing for someone doing retirement budget math is this: Asheville rewards homeowners and penalizes renters. If you arrive with equity from a previous home sale and purchase here outright, or close to it, the cost of living becomes manageable on a moderate fixed income. If you arrive planning to rent indefinitely while you figure out the real estate market, the math gets harder fast. The city's housing premium is real, the rental market is tight, and rents have risen considerably over the past five years as the metro's population has grown. Know which situation you are walking into before you get here.

The Silver Tsunami Is Not a Metaphor

Buncombe County's senior population is growing faster than almost any other demographic, and the scale of the shift is striking enough that it deserves more than a passing mention. During the pandemic years of 2020 through 2022, adults over 65 accounted for 96.1 percent of the county's population growth. Today, 22.6 percent of Buncombe County residents are older than 65. By 2036, projections suggest one in four residents will belong to that cohort. As of the most recent Census data, 19.25 percent of the City of Asheville's population is 65 or older.

This is why the pickleball courts are full at 9 a.m. on a Tuesday. It is why there are waitlists at retirement communities. It is also, from the perspective of someone considering a move, one of the more underappreciated arguments for coming here — and, admittedly, a reason the traffic has gotten noticeably worse.

What a large, active, engaged senior population produces in a city is infrastructure and culture that actually serves older adults rather than treating them as an afterthought. Asheville has developed a density of senior centers, lifelong learning programs, hiking groups organized by pace rather than age, arts communities with meaningful participation from people over 60, and volunteer organizations where institutional knowledge and available time create genuinely effective civic work. The Osher Lifelong Learning Institute at UNC Asheville offers peer-taught college-level courses to adults 50 and over, with no grades and no tests. The class on Appalachian history fills within hours of registration opening. The one on French cinema takes slightly longer.

The social fabric that a large senior population weaves is not always visible from the outside, but it is one of the things that residents cite most consistently when asked why they stay. If you move somewhere and everyone your age is still working and commuting, the city is effectively unavailable to you during the hours when you are most free. Asheville does not have that problem. The city is engaged and accessible in the middle of a Tuesday in a way that most American cities are not. This is either a feature or a warning sign about the local economy. Probably both.

The demand for aging services has strained county resources, and it would be dishonest to pretend otherwise. County funding for senior services has stagnated at roughly $2 million annually for the past several years while the population requiring those services has grown substantially. Transportation assistance, in-home care coordination, and nutrition programs are all oversubscribed. But this is a governance and funding problem, not a quality-of-life problem for most people who move here independently and in reasonable health. The strain affects the most vulnerable residents most directly. If you are arriving at 62 in good health with your financial situation sorted out, the silver tsunami is much more likely to feel like your community than your burden.

Why the Rankings Keep Coming

US News and World Report has ranked Asheville number 4 among the Best Places to Retire. SmartAsset's 2025 study ranked Buncombe County seventh in North Carolina for retirement, citing 4.83 medical centers per 1,000 people, favorable tax treatment, and social opportunities. These rankings are deeply inconvenient if your goal is to prevent people from moving here. They keep appearing anyway.

The rankings reflect a genuine calculation: a mild four-season climate where snow is a seasonal event rather than an eight-month ordeal, extraordinary natural beauty accessible within minutes of town, an engaged and eclectic cultural scene that rarely feels like something designed for a demographic, no state tax on Social Security, and a healthcare infrastructure that, despite its current turbulence, remains more developed than what you will find in most comparably sized mountain cities anywhere in the country.

The healthcare turbulence is real. The accountability effort is real. And the competitive expansion that may, within a few years, give residents genuine alternatives is also real. All three things are true simultaneously.

What Healthcare Actually Looks Like Day to Day

This chapter has covered a lot of ground, and deliberately so. A decision about where to retire is not just a decision about hospitals. It is a decision about where you will live, what you can afford, what kind of community you want around you, and what happens if your health needs change over the next twenty or thirty years. All of that belongs in the same chapter because all of it is the same decision. The healthcare infrastructure shapes the neighborhood choices. The neighborhood choices affect the cost of living. The cost of living determines whether the retirement communities are accessible. And the retirement communities are, for many people, the backstop that makes the whole thing work. You cannot make a good decision about any one of those pieces without understanding the others. Now that you have the full picture, the actual question most people are asking is this: what does it feel like, day to day, to navigate healthcare here as a relatively healthy person in your 60s or 70s?

The honest answer is: largely fine, with some friction at the edges. Primary care physicians are available and often excellent, particularly through MAHEC's clinics and the independent practices that have grown up around Mission's orbit. Specialists are more of a mixed picture. Cardiology, orthopedics, and oncology have multiple strong options. Other specialties that were decimated in the post-HCA exodus are harder to access locally, which means occasional drives to Greenville, Charlotte, or the UNC Medical Center in Chapel Hill for specific procedures or second opinions. This is not dramatically different from what you would experience in most small and mid-sized American cities, and it is considerably better than what rural Appalachian communities to the west are dealing with. It is simply worth knowing that 'major regional medical center' does not mean every subspecialty is conveniently available without travel.

For routine and preventive care, Asheville's infrastructure is genuinely strong. The city has multiple urgent care options for non-emergency needs that do not require an emergency room visit, which is where a lot of the Mission quality concerns become less relevant to daily life. Pardee in Hendersonville is a twenty-five-minute drive from most of south Asheville and increasingly functions as a parallel system for the kinds of procedures and follow-up visits that do not require Mission's trauma or specialty capabilities. Many Asheville-area residents have quietly reorganized their healthcare around Pardee for everything that does not specifically require Mission, and Pardee has responded by expanding its south Asheville outreach.

The veterans in the room have an entirely different and considerably more favorable story. The Charles George VA on Tunnel Road is a full-service facility offering a comprehensive range of specialties, and VA healthcare by its nature insulates you from most of the commercial healthcare market's dysfunction. But the Charles George VA is not merely adequate. It is, by several independent measures, one of the best-performing VA facilities in the country. For fiscal year 2025, it earned first place on the VA's SAIL scorecard, with an Overall Hospital Rating of 95.1 percent against a national average of 73.4 percent. The Centers for Medicare and Medicaid Services has awarded it a five-star rating for two consecutive years. It has ranked number one for Best Place to Work in the VA system's All Employee Survey in four of the last six years, which turns out to matter: hospitals where staff want to work tend to be hospitals where patients want to be treated. Veterans who moved to Asheville specifically because of the VA's reputation here tend to have the most straightforwardly positive accounts of the local healthcare experience, and the data supports them.

The bottom line for a healthy person in their 60s making a retirement move: identify a primary care physician before you arrive, or within the first month. Establish care with Pardee as a secondary option for non-emergency needs. Know where the nearest urgent care is from your home. Have a conversation with your primary care doctor early on about which specialists they trust locally and which needs might require a Charlotte or Chapel Hill trip. This is not a complicated plan. It is the same plan thoughtful people execute in any mid-sized American city. The difference in Asheville is that the stakes of not having a plan feel slightly higher given Mission's current situation, but the resources available for executing a good plan are genuinely better than in most comparable mountain cities.

Anyone considering Asheville as a retirement destination deserves an honest accounting, and here it is. The mythology about small mountain hospitals and helicopter evacuations is wrong. Asheville has serious medical infrastructure. It has a Level I trauma center, a teaching hospital pipeline, a VA medical center, multiple regional hospitals within 30 to 45 minutes, a growing complement of competing systems that want a piece of the market, and a continuing care organization that was just ranked the best in North Carolina. You have now been warned.

What it also has is a flagship hospital run by a for-profit company whose track record of cutting staff while extracting profits has been exhaustively documented by journalists, academics, federal regulators, the state Attorney General, and the community's own coalition of physicians and nurses. The problems at Mission are not rumors or hyperbole. They are a matter of public record and ongoing regulatory scrutiny.

People ask whether they should factor Mission's problems into a decision to move here. The answer is yes, with context. The context is that healthcare systems change, competition changes them faster, and the regulatory and political pressure on HCA in Western North Carolina is unlike anything the company has faced in most of its other markets. The story is still being written.

If you are 55 and planning ahead, you have time to watch how the competitive landscape develops, particularly whether AdventHealth's Weaverville hospital ever actually breaks ground and what Novant's Certificate of Need application produces. If you are 75 and making a move now, the practical advice is to identify a primary care physician the moment you arrive, build a relationship with Pardee in Hendersonville as an alternative to Mission for non-emergency care, and understand that in a genuine emergency, Mission's Level I trauma designation means you will receive serious care even if the surrounding experience leaves something to be desired.

The infrastructure is here. The weather is exceptional. The mountains are not going anywhere. The question is whether you arrive with your eyes open about who controls the dominant healthcare institution, what the alternatives look like, and what your backup plans should be if the system stumbles while you need it most.

Most people who move here figure this out within six months, usually the hard way. You are now ahead of the curve. Try not to be smug about it.

CHAPTER SEVEN

DON'T MOVE HERE
IF YOU LIKE
SEEING THE HORIZON

Stand on Biltmore Avenue on a clear March morning in 2026 and try to find Mount Pisgah. It is out there. It has been out there for roughly 300 million years, patient as geology can afford to be. But between you and it there is now a 19-story tower of steel, glass, and synthetic stone rising 228 feet from the corner of Patton Avenue. It is called the Kimpton Hotel Arras, and it is doing what tall buildings do: commanding the skyline while everything behind it recedes politely. The person next to you is holding a Green Sage Cafe cup. She is also craning her neck. The comedy writes itself.

This is not a new problem. Cities have always grown in ways that rearranged the views their residents once took for granted. Rome built inward. Manhattan built up. Asheville, hemmed in by ridgelines on every side and blessed with more tourists per square mile than it can comfortably absorb, built hotels. What makes Asheville's version of this story distinctive is the speed, the terrain, and the particular flavor of irony involved. You moved to a mountain town to see mountains. The mountain town, it turns out, had other plans.

Asheville has solved an ancient civic riddle: how do you keep a mountain town authentic while also charging $38 for a two-pour whiskey flight? The answer is: you don't solve it. You build tall enough that the people who can see the mountains are already paying for the privilege. Welcome to vertical Asheville, a city that ran out of horizontal room somewhere around 2021 and decided to simply go skyward, one Edison-bulb rooftop bar at a time.

This chapter is about what happens when a city is too successful for its own good. It is about a place so desirable that the machinery built to welcome visitors ends up remaking the skyline entirely. The hotels are, in that sense, just the part you can see from the street. Everything else is underneath them.

Why Asheville Grows Like a Teenager: Only Up

Before Asheville imposed its hotel construction moratorium in September 2019, the city had approximately 8,564 hotel rooms. By 2023, that number had climbed to roughly 9,119. When the moratorium was lifted in February 2021, nearly 1,700 additional rooms were either under construction or in the development pipeline, representing an 18% projected increase in hotel inventory arriving in under three years. To put that in mountain-town terms: Asheville was growing its hotel inventory by the equivalent of a mid-sized Holiday Inn every single year.

The moratorium itself was a fascinating civic exercise. The city pressed pause on hotel construction because it had noticed, with some alarm, that it was becoming a city of hotels. Developers, interpreting the pause as a signal that the window was closing, spent the moratorium years doing paperwork. When the window reopened, the pipeline was full. The pause had the unintended effect of concentrating hotel development rather than limiting it, which is exactly the kind of outcome that gives urban planners insomnia.

The geography is not an excuse. It is the whole explanation.

Unlike Charlotte, which can sprawl horizontally into the Piedmont for approximately forever, Asheville sits in a bowl. The city's own zoning code acknowledges this with admirable understatement, noting that "Asheville is in a unique geographic location where mountains, valleys, and hills constitute significant natural topographic features." Steep-slope ordinances restrict development on any grade exceeding 15%, which eliminates vast tracts of surrounding hillside from consideration. When you cannot build out, you build up. When you build up in a tourism economy, you build hotels.

When Asheville lifted the moratorium, it revised its zoning to create overlay districts that funneled new hotel development into specific corridors: downtown, the River Arts District, Biltmore Village, and Tunnel Road. The result is a concentrated vertical stack in the exact places visitors walk. The mountain views that once greeted a tourist stepping out of a gallery on Lexington Avenue are now replaced, in several directions, by the blank glass flank of whatever project arrived last in the pipeline. This is called managed growth. It manages remarkably well for the hotels.

The Moxy Asheville broke ground in November 2022 and opened on September 13, 2024, fourteen days before Hurricane Helene. It sits on Biltmore Avenue, six floors, 115 rooms. On the seventh floor is Wildwood Still, offering more than 150 whiskeys, Asian-inspired small plates, and fire pits overlooking what the hotel's marketing describes as "unbeatable Blue Ridge Mountain views." They are, objectively, excellent views. They are one story above where the views used to be free. The Moxy is the first Marriott-branded Moxy property in North Carolina. It will not be the last anything in Asheville.

The Flat Iron Hotel tells a more complicated story. The historic Flat Iron Building at Battery Park Avenue and

Wall Street was constructed in 1926 and spent most of its life as one of the last repositories of affordable, accessible, non-gentry downtown space: independent offices, arts organizations, and Sky Bar, which occupied the eighth floor and asked nothing of you beyond being alive and present in Asheville. In 2019, a developer proposed converting it to a boutique hotel. City Council blocked the proposal.

By May 2024, after a five-year renovation, the hotel opened anyway: 71 rooms, an Italian-Appalachian restaurant called Luminosa, an underground speakeasy, a co-working space called Iron Works, and a rooftop bar with panoramic views of downtown and the Great Smoky Mountains. The council blocking it in 2019 bought the building five years of being what it was. Then it became what it was going to become regardless.

There is also the matter of what may become the single largest structure in downtown Asheville. A proposed 313-room addition to the existing Four Points Sheraton, attached to the current structure, was described in a 2023 analysis as potentially encompassing roughly 480,000 square feet. City Council approved it. When built, it will dwarf everything around it by most physical measures. It will, of course, be described as boutique.

The community's response to the general trajectory was captured with unusual precision by a 2023 Reddit thread discussing a proposed 20-story hotel project downtown. One comment offered: "Bend over Asheville, council is about to insert a 20-story hotel right into your downtown." An elected council member responded with something more measured but no less pointed: "There's a tale of two Ashevilles, one where outside investors and owning-class neighbors are from our tourism industry, and another where working poor renters and households vulnerable to gentrification are displaced by unchecked tourism." This was not a fringe voice from the internet. It was an elected official, at a council meeting, describing her own city. The room did not push back. The construction continued.

Building the World's Most Beautiful Stage for a 48-Hour Audience

Visitors to Buncombe County pay a 6% occupancy tax on every hotel and short-term rental stay. In the 2021-2022 fiscal year, that generated $37.5 million in occupancy tax revenue, the third-highest total in North Carolina. A portion of that revenue, boosted in 2022 when state legislation increased the community capital allocation from one-quarter to one-third, flows into the Legacy Investment from Tourism Fund, known locally and in grant applications as the LIFT Fund.

The LIFT Fund's first funding cycle invested nearly $10 million across twelve community projects in 2024. The full project list is worth reading carefully, because it is a precise document of civic priorities expressed in dollar amounts.

Coxe Avenue Complete Street, a pedestrian infrastructure project, received $2,983,890. The Harrah's Cherokee Center arena received $675,000. The Blue Ridge Parkway Foundation's Craggy Gardens Visitor Center project received $750,000. The Hood Huggers Foundation's Blue Note Junction project received $500,000. Ferry Road affordable housing received $4,000,000, for the recreational components only, meaning the greenways and trails adjacent to the development, not the housing itself. Aston Park Tennis Center received $40,000. The Asheville Botanical Garden received $150,000.

Sit with the Ferry Road line for a moment. Four million dollars went to the walking paths surrounding an affordable housing development. The largest single investment in the LIFT Fund's first cycle went to the amenities around housing rather than the housing itself. This is not cynicism. It is the fund doing precisely what its governance structure was designed to produce.

The committee that decides how LIFT money is spent must, by law, be composed of a majority of owners or operators of hotels, motels, or other taxable lodging accommodations. The people who generate the most tourist foot traffic hold formal oversight authority over where the tourist money goes. Nearly $3 million going to pedestrian streetscaping on Coxe Avenue, so visitors can walk more pleasantly between the six-story boutique hotels, is not an accident. It is a committee making rational decisions in its own interest, which committees reliably do. Calling this a conflict of interest would be uncharitable. Calling it governance would be accurate.

Explore Asheville calls the underlying model the "Virtuous Visitor Cycle" in its official materials. The argument: marketing inspires visitor spending; lodging tax funds the marketing; 70% of visitor spending occurs outside lodging, meaning restaurants, shops, and attractions all benefit. This is internally consistent. It is also a closed loop that optimizes for the 48-hour visitor who arrives, eats at a farm-to-table restaurant, buys a $65 hand-dyed hoodie, and leaves before the traffic on I-26 backs up on Sunday afternoon. The person who made the hoodie, who has lived in Asheville for twelve years, is not a variable in the Virtuous Visitor Cycle. She is an externality.

The Virtuous Visitor Cycle has a shadow economy running alongside it. Short-term rentals, the Airbnbs and VRBOs that have colonized residential neighborhoods across Buncombe County, feed the same loop. By 2022, there were 5,268 short-term rentals in Buncombe County, accounting for roughly 4.5% of the county's total housing stock. Short-term rental revenue in the county grew from $18.7 million in 2016 to $229 million in 2022, an increase of more than 1,000% in six years. Every one of those units is a house or apartment that a long-term resident is not living in.

The City of Asheville moved first. In 2018, the City Council voted 6-1 to ban short-term rentals of entire homes in most residential zones, limiting the practice to homestays of one or two rooms in owner-occupied properties. The county, which has jurisdiction only over unincorporated areas outside city limits, spent most of 2024 trying to follow suit. The Buncombe County Planning Board held three public listening sessions, fielded emotional testimony from service workers, retirees, and neighborhood advocates, and drafted and redrafted proposed restrictions on new short-term rentals in single-family residential zones. Airbnb responded by emailing its local hosts urging them to attend meetings and contact county officials. The board postponed its vote in April 2024 to allow further study. The housing stock continued to shrink while the study was conducted.

One planning board member put the underlying tension plainly: "We cannot allow a situation where we are constantly addressing the needs of tourists and not addressing the needs of our own people." The county's own analysis found that the 5,268 short-term rental units accounted for roughly 68% of the long-term rental housing gap identified in the 2021 Dogwood Health Trust study. This is what the Virtuous Visitor Cycle looks like from the inside of a neighborhood: the TDA markets Asheville to visitors, visitors demand places to stay, homeowners convert residential properties to short-term rentals to meet that demand, long-term rental supply contracts, workers cannot find housing, and the TDA markets Asheville to more visitors. The cycle is virtuous for someone. The question is who.

The next LIFT Fund cycle opens in Spring 2026. It will, in

all probability, contain more wayfinding signage. The signage will be tasteful. The fonts will be on-brand.

The Rooftop Bar Industrial Complex

By early 2026, the downtown Asheville rooftop bar is no longer a novelty. It is infrastructure. It is the thing the city builds when it has run out of horizontal surface and needs somewhere to put the fire pits. There are enough of them now that a visitor could, theoretically, spend an entire weekend moving from one to the next without ever descending to street level. Several visitors have done exactly this. They report the views are excellent.

A partial inventory, current as of this writing: Soprana Rooftop Cucina, perched on the seventh floor of the Embassy Suites on Haywood Street, offers westward views of the Blue Ridge and is described in multiple early 2026 write-ups as offering possibly the best panorama among all of Asheville's rooftop options; reservations are handled through Resy. The Montford Rooftop Bar, on the eighth floor of the DoubleTree by Hilton on Haywood Street, offers stellar mountain views, opens daily at 4 PM, and includes free valet parking, which is now a rooftop bar amenity, in the same category as good lighting and a working heat lamp. Pillar Bar at the Hilton Garden Inn offers garden-to-glass craft cocktails, fire pits, greenery, and live music several nights a week.

VISUALS Wine and Cocktail Bar, positioned above Eulogy Music Hall, offers natural wines and aperitifs with what its materials describe as a connection to the arts scene, which is a description that could mean almost anything. Capella on 9 is noted in community reviews as "a tad pricey," with service described as needing improvement, which is the polite way of saying you waited 22 minutes for a drink while watching the Blue Ridge turn pink. The Flat Iron Hotel's rooftop offers panoramic views of downtown and the Great Smoky Mountains from the same building that, five years ago, housed Sky Bar, which you reached by walking in off the street.

There is also a business called Asheville Rooftop Bar Tours, founded in 2018, which offered guided walking tours with reserved seating at multiple downtown rooftop venues per evening. The company's marketing language promised sweeping views of the Blue Ridge Mountains and down-town skyline in refined settings that transform an ordinary evening into something extraordinary. After Hurricane Helene, the tours had not resumed. Even the tour of the rooftops went dark.

The Sky Bar deserves its own paragraph, and probably a small plaque, and if we are being honest about it, a brief moment of silence before we move on.

It occupied the eighth floor of the Flat Iron Building, at the corner of Battery Park Avenue and Wall Street, and it was not fancy by any measurable standard. The elevator was slow. The furniture was the kind that accumulates in a place over years rather than being selected by a designer. The bar itself was not architectural. It was a bar. What it had, and what nothing in its price category had anywhere else in downtown Asheville, was the view: the Blue Ridge rolling west in the late afternoon light, the kind of panorama that reminds you, whether you want to be reminded or not, that you are living inside something genuinely extraordinary.

There was no minimum spend. No reservation system. No charcuterie board constructed to justify a ticket price. You walked in off Battery Park Avenue, took an elevator that moved at the pace of a reasonable conversation, and arrived on the eighth floor with whatever drink you ordered from the bar at prices that did not require you to do arithmetic before deciding. A local graphic designer might sit across from a tourist from Columbus, Ohio. Neither of them had booked anything. Both of them were looking at the same mountains. For the duration of a drink, they were, without any policy framework requiring it, sharing the same city.

That experience sounds unremarkable when you describe it. That is the point. It was unremarkable. It was the kind of thing a functioning city produces without trying: a public-facing space, accessible without a reservation, where the view belongs to whoever shows up. Asheville had one of those, in one of its most iconic buildings, in the middle of its most visited downtown corridor. It had it until May 2024, when the Flat Iron Hotel opened and the Sky Bar did not.

The Flat Iron Hotel's rooftop bar is objectively lovelier in every design sense. The lighting is better. The napkins are pressed linen. The cocktail menu references the local terrain with appropriate reverence and a $17 price point. The view is panoramic. The view is, in fact, the same view. What changed is the system through which you access it. If you are a hotel guest, you reach the rooftop from the lobby. If you are not a hotel guest, you are welcome to make a dinner reservation at Luminosa, the Italian-Appalachian restaurant on the ground floor, where entrées start at $28 and the rooftop becomes accessible after your meal. If you are a local graphic designer who used to ride the slow elevator between client calls, you can still get there. It just costs more, takes longer, and requires you to want dinner.

The view is the same. The access is different. That is, in four words, the whole story of what happened to downtown Asheville between 2019 and 2026.

The mountains are free. They have been free for 300 million years. They were free when Zebulon Vance was governor, free when Thomas Wolfe was drafting his complaints about the place and planning his escape, and free on the morning of September 27, 2024, when the French Broad River rose thirty feet and rearranged the lower city with no input from the zoning board. The mountains remain. But to see them from inside the city that sits among them, you now need a credit card, a reservation, and a willingness to drink something called "The Graveyard Fields" while a fire pit blows cedar-scented smoke in your direction. The Buncombe Turnpike hog drovers of the 1820s pushed 150,000 pigs through this same valley and left more usable infrastructure behind them. At least the hogs did not require valet parking.

Every Brick Wall Must Be Distressed

There is a design language that follows hotel development like a shadow, and by 2026 it has colonized every surface of downtown Asheville. It is a language of curated authenticity, and it is remarkably consistent across properties, price points, and ownership structures. Walk into any new hotel lobby in the district and you will find yourself inside the same aesthetic, with slightly different light fixtures.

Every original brick wall must be exposed. Every lightbulb must be an Edison filament. Every cocktail must reference local geography: "The Graveyard Fields," "The Bearwallow," "Lover's Leap Mule," "The Craggy Gardens." Every staff member must be tattooed in a manner that suggests they were once in a band, or perhaps still are on weekends. Every menu must contain the word "sourced," ideally multiple times and with increasing specificity. Every hotel lobby must smell faintly of cedar and ambition. Every check-in desk must be made from reclaimed wood, the provenance of which is available upon request.

The Foundry Hotel is, in this respect, the original text. Developers converted a 1915 industrial steel-casting site into an 87-room Hilton Curio Collection property. The building's industrial bones, exposed steel, original brick, timber beams, were kept and celebrated. The restaurant on the ground floor is called The Refinery. It was previously Benne on Eagle, named for The Block.

The Block was Asheville's Black Wall Street. Centered on Eagle and South Market Streets, just south of Pack Square, it emerged in the late nineteenth century as one of the most vital African American commercial districts in the South, home to hundreds of Black-owned businesses: grocery stores, barbershops, nightclubs, restaurants, boarding houses, and professional offices. It has been recognized as the nation's oldest continuously operating African American commercial district. Its anchor institution, the YMI Cultural Center, was founded in 1893 with partial funding from George Vanderbilt, who needed housing for the Black laborers building his estate and provided capital for an institution that would outlast him by more than a century. The Block flourished because it had to. Segregation meant Black residents could not patronize white-owned businesses downtown. They built their own economy instead, and for decades it thrived.

Then urban renewal arrived. Beginning in the late 1950s and continuing through the 1980s, city-directed redevelopment demolished homes, displaced residents, and shuttered businesses across the district. The mechanism was bureaucratic and the results were catastrophic. A community that had built itself from nothing, in circumstances designed to prevent exactly that, was dismantled by the same civic apparatus that had ignored it for generations. One longtime Asheville resident noted that meaningful investment in the area came only after the community composition became predominantly white, a timeline that speaks for itself.

Today, the Eagle Market Streets Development Corporation, a nonprofit anchored in the district, has developed 62 units of affordable housing and more than 16,000 square feet of commercial and community space. After Hurricane Helene, it activated its properties as emergency relief hubs. The Block is coming back, on its own terms, with its own people. It does not need a hotel to tell its story.

The Foundry Hotel is genuinely good. The food at The Refinery is genuinely good. The authenticity of the industrial conversion is real and documented. None of that is the point. The point is that a Hilton Curio Collection property now commercially benefits from proximity to a history it did not create, did not protect, and did not mourn when it was being dismantled. The restaurant is named for what was lost. The hotel is named for what replaced it. Both names are accurate. Only one of them required an architectural firm.

The Bank of America Building on Patton Avenue came down in August 2020 to make way for a six-story, 60-room boutique hotel. The developer explained what distinguished this project from the hotels people were protesting: "What makes this hotel different is that it is boutique." It is not clear at what room count a boutique hotel stops being a boutique hotel and starts being simply a hotel. The threshold appears to be always one higher than the current proposal.

In 2019, the Asheville Blade documented a proposed hotel project that would have displaced nearly 80 local businesses and organizations from a single downtown building, described as one of "the last non-gentry business and organizational space in downtown Asheville." City Council blocked that specific project. The pattern it represented, small offices, music rehearsal spaces, nonprofits, and odd-hour services losing ground floor by floor to hospitality development, continued without interruption through the following six years, through the moratorium, through

Helene, and into 2026.

One Reddit commenter, responding to news of the Flat Iron Hotel's opening in 2024, offered an eleven-word forecast: "This town is going to have so many hotels there won't be anything to visit anymore." The comment was written as a complaint. It reads, two years later, more like a question that has not yet been fully answered.

The True Survivors

Hurricane Helene made landfall on September 27, 2024. Within days, Asheville had no water, no cell service, no power, and no tourists. About 40 downtown businesses had closed by mid-2025. The average small business in the region lost $322,000. Hospitality employment in the Asheville metro dropped more than 7% year over year by September 2025. Fiscal year 2025, July 2024 through June 2025, saw a 23% decline in lodging sales countywide. Forty-seven percent of business owners reported they were struggling financially a year after the storm.

And yet.

The hotels did not close. Not a single one. They posted reduced rates, adjusted staffing, and waited. That is the thing about a structure built with institutional capital, a national brand, and a ten-year debt instrument: it can afford to wait. The French Broad River destroyed dozens of small businesses along its banks in a single afternoon. The glass-and-steel hotel boxes uphill from the floodplain remained dry, functional, and bookable.

By January 2026, hotel occupancy in Asheville and Buncombe County had recovered to 63%. Ed Silver, vice president of business development for Explore Asheville, reported at the January 28, 2026 Tourism Development Authority meeting that this performance was "stronger than many comparable markets amid a nationwide decline in hotel bookings." Forward bookings for July through December 2026 were up 38% compared to the same period in 2025. Silver was careful to note that 63% is not a number to celebrate outright. It is a number to contextualize. In the current national hotel environment, it is, apparently, respectable.

In Fiscal Year 2025, group and meetings travel booked through Explore Asheville generated $67.4 million in direct spending, a 35% increase over the prior year, while group room bookings grew 39% to 115,393 room nights. This happened in the fiscal year that included the storm, the water outage, and four months during which the city was effectively closed to visitors. The meetings and convention business, operating on a longer booking horizon than leisure travel, had made its commitments before Helene and largely honored them after.

This is the hotels' structural advantage. They are the most disaster-resistant entity in the post-Helene economy. A small business that loses four months of revenue closes. A 115-room Marriott-branded hotel with national reservations systems, corporate recovery infrastructure, institutional insurance coverage, and brand loyalty programs measured in hundreds of millions of enrolled members loses four months of revenue and then posts 38% forward bookings before the debris is fully cleared from the River Arts District. The river took everything that was soft. The glass-and-steel hotel boxes on Biltmore Avenue hummed back to life like air conditioners after a summer thunderstorm, which is not a metaphor anyone planned but which captures the situation precisely.

Governor Josh Stein traveled to a tourism conference in March 2026 to urge visitors to return to Western North Carolina. The state's tourism apparatus mobilized. Explore Asheville launched recovery campaigns. The message, broadly, was: Asheville is open. Come back. Spend money. The hotels were ready. The small businesses that survived were ready. The ones that did not survive were not there to receive the message, which is how recovery works in a tourism economy: the infrastructure that can wait comes back; the infrastructure that cannot wait does not.

The Moxy keeps coming up in this chapter because it is the most compressed version of everything this chapter is about: built fast, built tall, built to last, and entirely indifferent to what came before it and what came after. It opened fourteen days before the storm, which is either terrible timing or perfect timing depending on whether you measure by trauma or by balance sheets. The French Broad has been reshaping this valley since before the valley took its current form. The Moxy is roughly sixteen months old. Right now, the Moxy is winning on occupancy rates.

A Field Guide to the New Downtown

These are not complaints. These are documentation.

The Sky Bar Problem. You used to be able to walk into the Flat Iron Building, take an elevator to the eighth floor, and look at the mountains. No reservation. No minimum spend. No wristband or hotel key. You just needed to be alive and present in Asheville. The Flat Iron Hotel has a rooftop bar now. It is beautiful, with panoramic views of downtown and the Great Smoky Mountains. You can reach it from the lobby if you are a hotel guest. If you are a local graphic designer who used to duck up there between client calls, you are welcome to make a dinner reservation at Luminosa, where entrées start at $28. The mountains are the same mountains. The access is the thing that changed.

The Cocktail Naming Rights Racket. At some point between 2018 and 2024, every waterfall, trail, and mountain overlook in Western North Carolina was quietly annexed as a cocktail name. "The Graveyard Fields." "The Lover's Leap." "The Bearwallow Mule." These cocktails cost between $14 and $20. The actual Graveyard Fields on the Blue Ridge Parkway remains free, assuming the Parkway has not been closed for Helene-related landslide repairs, which at various points it has been. The cocktail named after the waterfall is available year-round. The waterfall has a more complicated schedule.

The Edison Bulb Emissions. A serious study should be conducted on the number of Edison filament bulbs installed in downtown Asheville between 2019 and 2026. The raw wattage of artisanal nostalgia lighting now illuminating hotel lobbies, rooftop bars, and boutique retail corridors across the district could, if redirected, probably power the Moxy's rooftop fire pits indefinitely. This would at least represent a form of sustainability, which the design briefs always mention.

The "Sourced" Menu Escalation. "Locally sourced." Then "hyper-locally sourced." Then "foraged." Then "foraged by our chef's neighbor, a guy named Daryl, who lives twenty minutes out past the fairgrounds." At the current rate of sourcing specificity, menus will list the emotional state of the mushroom picker within eighteen months, followed by the mushroom's preferred growing conditions and a brief biography of the mycelium network.

The Valet Parking Irony. At least three downtown rooftop bars now offer free valet parking as an amenity. This is not a joke. Free valet parking is listed alongside craft cocktails and Blue Ridge views as a reason to choose one rooftop bar over another. It exists because the city, having spent its development capacity on hotel towers rather than parking structures, has created a situation in which a car anywhere near downtown is a genuine problem, and the hospitality industry's solution to that problem is to hire someone young to deal with it.

Consider the valet. He is, let us say, twenty-three years old. He grew up in Weaverville, twenty minutes north. He works four nights a week parking cars for guests of a rooftop bar that charges $17 for a cocktail named after a waterfall he has visited on his days off because it is free. He arrives for his shift by bus, because parking near his workplace costs $14 for the evening and he will net $80 on a good night. He stands at the entrance in his branded vest and takes the keys from a couple who drove down from Asheville Park in a leased Audi. They are going up to the rooftop. He is going to move their car.

The journey of the Audi is its own small comedy. There is a surface lot two blocks east, but it fills by 6 PM on weekends. There is a city-owned deck on Rankin, but two of its four levels were closed for repair in early 2026. The valet knows three other valets from other rooftop bars who are also circling at this hour, each of them piloting someone else's vehicle through a downtown grid that was not designed for the volume of cars that the hotel development pipeline has now deposited at its edges. They pass each other occasionally. They wave. Eventually the Audi finds a spot in the deck on Lexington, eight minutes away on foot, which is fine because the valet is not walking back. He is jogging.

The couple on the rooftop orders The Bearwallow Mule and watches the Blue Ridge go pink in the last of the evening light. The service is seamless. The parking was free. The valet returns to the stand, slightly out of breath, and takes the next set of keys. This is being marketed as a luxury hospitality experience. It is not wrong to call it that. It is also a precise diagram of a city that solved its horizontal infrastructure problem by turning it into someone's job.

The Boutique Hotel Arms Race. Every new hotel is a boutique hotel. The 115-room Moxy is boutique. The 71-room Flat Iron is boutique. The 313-room addition to the Four Points Sheraton will presumably be boutique in some dimension not yet visible from street level. At what point does "boutique" stop meaning anything other than "expensive, and also there is an accent wall in the lobby"? The industry has declined to establish a ceiling, which is the right call commercially and the wrong call for the English language.

The "Community Space" Clause. The city's hotel development point system gives bonus credit to developers who include community spaces in their designs. This is a real policy mechanism with real consequences, the most predictable of which is the Moxy Hotel lobby.

The Moxy's community space consists of a state-of-the-art video wall, a grab-and-go market, and open seating described in the hotel's materials as designed for "creativity and connection." Community access is available during regular business hours, which are also check-in hours, which are the hours during which hotel guests arrive from the airport with rolling carry-ons and move through the lobby in the unpredictable lateral patterns of people who are not quite sure where anything is yet. The community member who has come to use the community space as a community space must navigate all of this to reach the couch near the video wall, which is currently occupied by a family from Raleigh waiting on their room to be ready.

Imagine you are a freelance illustrator who lives six blocks away on Biltmore Avenue. You have a deadline and your apartment is loud and the coffee shop on Lexington has a line. You arrive at 2 PM on a Wednesday with your laptop bag and a reasonable expectation that this is, by the city's own policy framework, a place where you are supposed to be. You push through the glass door. A luggage cart the approximate dimensions of a queen mattress is parked directly across the entrance. A hotel associate in a branded vest smiles at you warmly and asks if you're checking in. You explain that you are not. He gestures toward the seating area near the video wall, where the video wall is currently displaying a promotional loop about Asheville's waterfall trails. You sit down. A rolling suitcase clips your ankle. Someone asks if this seat is taken. It is taken. You are taking it. You are the community.

The grab-and-go market offers a $9 granola bar and a $7 cold brew. You buy the cold brew because you need the caffeine and because it feels vaguely subversive to spend money in a hotel lobby without booking a room. The video wall transitions to a loop about Asheville's dining scene. A couple with a Patagonia bag asks you if the hotel has a rooftop bar. You tell them it does. You tell them it is excellent. You have never been to it. You live here. The community space has functioned exactly as designed: it has created a connection between the hotel and the community. The connection is that the community is sitting in the hotel lobby being gently reminded that the rooftop bar exists.

The Distressed Brick Paradox. The boutique aesthetic requires that every surface appear authentically old. The irony is that many of the buildings demolished to make room for these authentically old-looking new structures were, in fact, genuinely old. Actual aging brick was replaced by brick that has been treated to look like it has aged. Authentic industrial patina was replaced by designed industrial patina. The result is visually identical to the original, except the ceiling is higher, the cocktail list is longer, and the monthly rate is different. Authenticity, in this context, is a finish. Not a history.

The Occupancy Tax Feedback Loop. Visitors pay a 6% occupancy tax. That tax funds marketing that attracts more visitors, who pay more occupancy tax, which funds more marketing. The committee overseeing that tax is legally required to be composed primarily of hotel owners and operators. The wayfinding signage on Coxe Avenue, funded in part by the same occupancy tax, allows visitors to walk more efficiently from one rooftop bar to the next. The signage is tasteful. The fonts are on-brand. Everyone is pointed in the right direction.

The View From the Ground. A longtime downtown resident described the shift as precisely as anyone has managed: "Downtown used to be a place where locals thrived, while visitors came to enjoy the unique essence of Asheville. At some point, the downtown area transformed into a mere representation of what Asheville is for tourists." This observation was posted on Reddit. It has not been refuted.

The Curated City

There is a woman who has lived in Asheville since 2009. She drives through downtown on a Tuesday afternoon in March 2026, looking for a parking spot that costs less than $3 an hour, squinting between two six-story buildings to catch a glimpse of Mount Pisgah. She cannot find the mountain or the parking. Both are there. Both have been there considerably longer than the buildings blocking them. Mount Pisgah has been there for 300 million years and will be there long after every Edison bulb in the district has burned out, every LIFT Fund cycle has funded its wayfinding signage, and the last "Bearwallow Mule" has been served to someone who flew in from Charlotte for a long weekend and will write a very nice review.

The mountains do not track occupancy rates. They do not follow the 38% jump in forward bookings for the second half of 2026, or the $67.4 million in direct spending generated by group travel last fiscal year, or the 39% increase in group room bookings. The mountains are not boutique. They are not curated. They cannot be distressed, because they already have been, repeatedly, geologically, catastrophically, and they came back the same as before, which is the one trick geology has that hotel development does not.

The hotels are, in the end, the clearest expression of Asheville's ambition and its anxiety. They are the physical record of a city that cannot say no to the thing that sustains it. The visitor economy generates $2.65 billion in annual spending and simultaneously makes it nearly impossible for a schoolteacher, a nurse, or a person who makes boutique hot sauce and sells it at the River Arts District Saturday market to afford to live within ten miles of where they work. The city builds tall because the terrain demands it. It builds glass because glass is modern and easy to clean and photographs well in the golden hour. It faces west because the sunsets over the Blue Ridge are, objectively and without argument, still free.

For now.

The rooftop bars do not block the mountains. Not technically. You can still see them from the street, if you stand in the right place, at the right angle, between the right buildings, at the right time of day. The view is still there. It has always been there. But the rooftop bars do put a $75 minimum spend between you and a comfortable seat from which to appreciate it. The beauty of this place is accessible to everyone, in theory, from the sidewalk below. You just have to look up now, past the fire pits and the Edison bulbs and the cocktail named after the waterfall, to find it.

The waterfall does not have a minimum spend. It does not have valet parking. It does not smell like cedar and ambition, though the cedar is admittedly in the neighborhood. It has been here longer than the hotels, longer than the moratorium, longer than the LIFT Fund and the overlay districts and the development pipeline. It just keeps moving, the way water does, the way mountains do, the way cities do when they can no longer afford to stay the same.

CHAPTER EIGHT

DON'T MOVE HERE
IF YOU WANT TO FIT IN

There are cities where fitting in is easy. You find the right neighborhood, buy the right car, join the right gym, and after a few months you can pass for a local without anybody noticing the effort. Asheville, North Carolina is not that city.

Asheville will not ask you to fit in. It will not show you the mold. It does not have one. What it has instead is a dense, self-reinforcing cultural identity built on the premise that the odder you are, the more at home you will feel. The bumper stickers say "Keep Asheville Weird," and everyone treats that less as a slogan and more as a zoning ordinance.

So if your idea of a good Saturday afternoon involves blending seamlessly into a crowd of people who all think exactly the way you do, this is a terrible place to live. You will stick out in the most unsettling way: by being unremarkably normal. Nobody will say anything, but they will notice.

The Weird Is Structural

"Keep Asheville Weird" traces its ancestry to Austin, Texas, where the phrase originated around 2000 as a desperate, defensive plea to save indie record shops from big-box retail. Austin adopted it as a slogan. It eventually drifted into a lifestyle brand, a pleasant backdrop for breakfast tacos and tech workers performing eccentricity on weekends. If you are packing a Subaru in Austin expecting our bumper stickers to mean the same thing as yours, turn the car around.

Asheville's weirdness is not an aesthetic you can take off when you go to work. It is an epistemological argument baked into the ground. We didn't get it from marketing consultants. We got it from European modernists like Josef and Anni Albers, who fled the shuttered Bauhaus and arrived in the Swannanoa Valley with a mandate: that art is how you train a human brain to tolerate ambiguity. That is not a quirky weekend hobby. That is a foundational conviction about how thinking works.

The result is what you might call Appalachian Modernism: the highly unusual collision of deeply rooted mountain craft traditions with the most aggressive mid-century avant-garde thinking on the planet. The Rauschenberg Foundation, the Cunningham Trust, and the entire trajectory of American minimalism and noise music trace their lineage right back to our backyard. The college ran out of money and closed in 1957, which is exactly what genuinely radical institutions do. But the intellectual permission it granted never left the atmosphere.

So if you are moving here because you think "weird" means drinking a hazy IPA while wearing a vintage hat, understand that you are stepping into a long and demanding syllabus. We don't want your quirky aesthetic. We require your tolerance for ambiguity. If you do not have it, Austin is perfectly nice this time of year.

This is a city of roughly 95,000 people where the financial advisor might also be a weekend brewer with dreadlocks down to his shoulders, where the woman in line at the coffee shop is wearing a tiara and nobody looks up from their laptops, where you can encounter a man riding a 20-foot tall bicycle through downtown in a nun's habit and the most remarkable thing about it is how unremarkable it feels after the third time.

Fisher Stark Real Estate, not typically the most avant-garde of institutions, sums up the local culture with unusual candor: if you're too weird for Asheville, you're too weird. That is not a warning. It is a boast.

The street-level evidence starts the moment you arrive downtown. Asheville issues busking permits and maintains designated performance zones, which is the kind of thing a city does when street performance is not an eyesore to be managed but a feature to be defended. On a warm Friday evening you will walk two blocks of Lexington Avenue and encounter three entirely different genres of music, none of them overlapping, none of them apologizing for their existence. You will pass an improvisational living statue, side-step a touring acrobat filling a gap between bookings, and almost certainly have to navigate around someone who is simply too staggeringly talented to be playing outside but chose the concrete over a stage anyway.

Every Friday evening in Pritchard Park, the city's most famous inconvenience takes place: an improvisational hand-drumming circle that runs without a set list, without a headliner, and without a ticket price. The city tried to shut it down in 2006 following noise complaints. Rather than permanently eliminating it, the city negotiated a solution and the drums kept beating. That is how Asheville handles inconvenient culture: accommodation, not suppression. If the sound of a free outdoor drum circle rattling the windows of your condo sounds like a problem to you, do not sign the lease.

But the weirdness is not accidental. It has roots, and those roots go back almost a century, to a small, impoverished, impossibly influential school in the hills just east of town.

The Ghost of Black Mountain College

In 1933, a group of educators established Black Mountain College in the Swannanoa Valley, about 15 miles from downtown Asheville. The school had no grades, no majors, no formal lectures, and almost no money. What it had was a radical conviction: that the arts should sit at the center of any serious education, not as decoration or elective but as foundational practice.

The founders were not making an argument about art. They were making an argument about how thinking works. John Andrew Rice, the college's founding rector, believed that learning to make something with your hands and your judgment trained a kind of thinking that no lecture could replicate. The arts were not the point. The thinking was the point. This was a radical position in 1933 and remains a radical position now, which is why most institutions have continued to ignore it.

The roster of people who passed through Black Mountain College between 1933 and its closure in 1957 reads like a syllabus for the entire second half of the 20th century. Josef and Anni Albers arrived from the Bauhaus after Hitler shut it down, bringing European modernism directly to the American mountains. Merce Cunningham developed his revolutionary approach to dance there, working alongside John Cage, who was reconsidering what music could be. Robert Rauschenberg showed up as a student and helped reshape what a painting could include. Willem and Elaine de Kooning spent time there.

Buckminster Fuller tested his geodesic dome concepts on the campus, with students as his construction crew. The dome collapsed on the first attempt, which Fuller apparently took as useful data.

What made the school's influence disproportionate to its

size was the density of exchange it produced. When Cage was composing and Cunningham was choreographing and Rauschenberg was painting and Fuller was building in the same small valley, the collisions between disciplines produced ideas that none of them would have arrived at alone. It never had more than a few hundred students and never had financial stability. It closed in 1957 because it simply ran out of money, as genuinely radical institutions so often do.

But the president of Charlotte's Bechtler Museum of Modern Art has said what many scholars believe: there would be no modern art museum as we know it today without Black Mountain College. A tiny, perpetually broke school in the Blue Ridge Mountains helped define what American art would become. The Rauschenberg Foundation, the Cunningham Trust, the legacy of the Albers in American art education, the influence of Cage on music from minimalism to noise, all of it runs through those years in the Swannanoa Valley.

Its ghost did not leave the mountains. The intellectual permission it granted, the idea that unconventional thinking was not just tolerated but required, settled into the cultural atmosphere of the region. The Black Mountain College Museum and Arts Center in downtown Asheville keeps the legacy active through exhibitions, publications, and programming. It is one of the smaller museums in the city and one of the more intellectually serious ones. When people wonder why Asheville feels so creatively dense for a city its size, Black Mountain College is a large part of the answer.

The River Arts District: A Mile of Studios

The most tangible expression of Asheville's art culture is also its most concentrated: the River Arts District, a roughly mile-long stretch of former industrial buildings along the

French Broad River that houses the working studios of more than 300 artists.

This is not a gallery district in the conventional sense, where polished rooms display finished work behind glass and the price tags are printed small. The RAD is a working district. Potters, painters, weavers, glassblowers, sculptors, jewelers, woodturners, and printmakers work in spaces that once housed actual industry, and many of those studios are open to the public every day of the year. You can watch a glassblower pull a molten vessel from a furnace, argue with a jeweler about the merits of a particular stone, and buy a painting directly from the person who made it, all on the same afternoon.

The industrial bones of the district are part of what makes it work. These are not spaces designed for art. They are spaces adapted for it, with the rough edges left intact. The loading docks and freight doors and exposed brick and concrete floors that defined these buildings as warehouses and factories now define them as studios, and the effect is a kind of authenticity that is very hard to manufacture. You are in a place where things are actually made, not just displayed.

Walking through the RAD on a weekday morning is not a gallery experience. It is more like wandering through a working neighborhood where the work happens to be art. A potter is centering clay on a wheel with the door open and the radio on. A metalworker is grinding something in the next unit, and the sound carries. A painter is photographing a finished canvas in the morning light and waves you in if you stop and look.

Nobody is performing for you. They are working, and you are walking through it. This is not a curated experience. It is a community with open doors.

Every second Saturday, the district holds an Art Stroll, a rolling open house with a free trolley that loops between studios. It is one of those events that sounds like a mildly pleasant way to kill two hours and turns into a five-hour disappearance. Artists who are ordinarily working with their doors half-open throw them fully open, demos happen, conversations start, and the whole district becomes something between a neighborhood block party and a rolling exhibition.

The RAD's buildings include the Wedge Studios, a converted 1920s railroad foundry that has been an artist complex since 1994; the Phil Mechanic Building, a former cotton warehouse that now houses galleries and studios across multiple floors; and the Curve Studios, which concentrates ceramics, sculpture, and metalwork under one industrial roof. Pink Dog Creative at 344 Depot Street, one of the buildings that sustained only minimal damage and reopened quickly after Helene, is home to more than 30 working artists, two restaurants and a coffee shop.

Among them is Andrea Kulish Wilhelm, a first-generation Ukrainian-American who has operated Studio A there since 2013, creating pysanky: Ukrainian decorated eggs made using a centuries-old wax-resist dyeing technique that her mother taught her when she was five years old. Three of her pysanky are in the permanent collection of the Pysanka Museum in Kolomyia, Ukraine. The Asheville area's connection to craft pottery runs deep, with the region claiming a lineage in studio pottery and hand-built ceramics that stretches back generations.

What Helene Did, and What Happened Next

In late September 2024, Hurricane Helene moved through western North Carolina and left behind flooding that no living person in the region had seen before. The French

Broad River, which runs directly through the River Arts District, rose to levels not recorded in over a century. The lower portion of the RAD went under up to 24 feet of water.

The damage was comprehensive. Floodwaters destroyed or severely damaged more than 300 artist studios. The storm affected over 750 working artists, many of whom lost not just their workspace but their inventory, their equipment, and in some cases their income entirely.

What happened next is the part worth paying close attention to.

Peter Roux is a contemporary landscape painter who had worked in his studio on the second floor of Riverview Station for six years. His paintings of sky, water, and land are held in private and corporate collections across the country, and he had operated a small adjacent gallery with his wife Rachel called Sky + Ground Contemporary Art. When the flood came through, it obliterated his studio. He lost more than 50 works of art, four commissioned pieces that were nearly complete, prepped canvases, and years of accumulated supplies. He had been a professional artist for over 20 years. "For the first time in my career, I'm starting over again," he said.

What Roux said about the experience, though, goes beyond the loss. He described the storm as a catalyst, pulling an already close community of artists even tighter together. "It was a catalyst for bringing an already tight community, the community of artists and the RAD, even closer together," he said. The storm did not scatter the RAD's artists. It concentrated them. That is not what usually happens when a neighborhood absorbs catastrophic damage.

Jeffrey Burroughs, a fine jeweler and president of River Arts District Artists, the district's membership organization, described seeing the district underwater as overwhelming.

The shock, he said, lasted almost no time at all before action took over. Within days, the organization was coordinating cleanups, helping artists salvage work, organizing community meetings, and distributing stipends. A temporary downtown retail space called the RADA Outpost opened to give displaced artists a place to sell their work while their studios remained inaccessible.

By the summer of 2025, 350 artists were back working in the district. The upper portion of the RAD, which sits on higher ground, was fully reopened. Studios closer to the river were beginning to reopen as well. And rather than simply restore what existed before, the community began asking what they could build that would serve artists better in the long term.

The River Arts District Artists Foundation moved in early 2026 to acquire a four-acre campus on Lyman Street, a 30,000-square-foot facility designed to be permanently flood-safe. The plan calls for affordable studio space built to keep working artists in Asheville for generations, not just for the next weather event.

Burroughs put it plainly: this is not just recovery. It is, in his words, a creative renaissance. They are not rebuilding what was there. They are reimagining it.

That word choice matters. A city that responded to catastrophic flooding by deciding to rebuild smarter and more inclusively is telling you something about its character.

The Numbers Behind the Art

Art is often discussed as though it were a pleasant supplement to a city's real economy, the kind of thing you fund when there's money left over. Asheville's numbers suggest a different relationship.

The Asheville metro area has more than 300 arts, culture,

and humanities nonprofits, collectively employing over 1,000 people and generating significant revenue annually. ArtsAVL, the county arts council, distributed more than $1.4 million in emergency relief grants to artists in the aftermath of Helene. In late 2025, it awarded Grassroots Arts grants to 49 local nonprofits across Buncombe County.

The 2026 ArtsAVL studies on the creative economy show an expected post-Helene slowdown, which is not surprising. What is notable is the infrastructure that exists to measure, respond to, and support that sector in a way that most mid-sized American cities simply do not have. Asheville treats its creative economy as an economy, not an amenity.

This is worth understanding before you move here. The arts are not a pleasant supplement to Asheville's real economy, not a weekend amenity you get to enjoy as a new resident. They are load-bearing. They are the structural core that gives the city its identity and therefore its economic buoyancy. The real estate you will pay top dollar for, the restaurants that will take your money on a Tuesday night, the cultural density that made you want to move here in the first place: all of it is underwritten by this ecosystem. If you complain about the cost of living while enjoying the benefits of a city built on the arts, you are missing the point entirely.

The Live Music Infrastructure

Asheville's music scene is worth its own discussion, separate from the festivals. The city has a live music infrastructure that is disproportionate to its size, built around a network of independent venues that have managed to survive the economic pressures that have closed similar rooms in larger cities.

The Orange Peel on Biltmore Avenue is the anchor. It opened in 2002 and has been named one of the top rock clubs in America by Rolling Stone. Its main room holds about 1,000 people and its booking history reads like a catalog of acts that were either already significant or became significant shortly after playing there. For a venue in a city of 95,000 people, its reputation is nationally outsized.

Around the Orange Peel, an ecosystem of smaller rooms, listening bars, and outdoor stages fills in the gaps. The Grey Eagle in the RAD books Americana, folk, and indie acts with serious regional credibility. The Isis Music Hall in West Asheville combines a concert venue with a restaurant. The Salvage Station, an outdoor venue along the French Broad River, was damaged by Helene and working toward recovery as of 2026. Between these rooms and the regular rotation of shows at breweries, hotel bars, and community spaces, the number of live music options on any given weekend in Asheville is notable.

The busking culture downtown adds another layer. The city's permitting system for street performers means that the sidewalks on a Saturday evening function as an informal secondary venue, with musicians working Lexington Avenue, Wall Street, and the areas around Pack Square. The quality ranges from students to touring musicians filling gaps between bookings, and occasionally to people who are simply very good and have chosen to play outside rather than inside.

The Galleries Beyond the RAD

The River Arts District gets most of the headlines, but Asheville's gallery scene extends considerably beyond a mile of riverfront studios.

The Asheville Art Museum, which reopened in 2019 after a major renovation and expansion in Pack Square Park downtown, anchors the city's institutional art world. Its permanent collection focuses on American art of the 20th and 21st centuries, with particular strength in works connected to Black Mountain College. The building itself is a significant piece of civic architecture in a downtown that takes design more seriously than most small cities do.

The Folk Art Center, operated by the Southern Highland Craft Guild on the Blue Ridge Parkway just east of downtown, is one of the oldest and most respected craft galleries in the Southeast. The Guild was established in 1930 and has been promoting and selling the traditional and contemporary crafts of the Southern Appalachians ever since. The Center's Allanstand Craft Shop is one of the oldest continuously operating craft shops in the country. The permanent collection includes over 4,000 objects in clay, fiber, glass, wood, and metal.

The Blue Spiral 1 Gallery on Biltmore Avenue has operated since 1991 and represents over 100 southeastern artists across painting, sculpture, ceramics, glass, and jewelry. It is one of the more significant commercial galleries in the region by both scale and longevity, and it has managed something that many galleries of its size do not: it has outlasted multiple cycles of the art market without abandoning its regional focus.

Momentum Gallery at 52 Broadway Street downtown occupies 15,000 square feet across two levels in a renovated Art Deco building and focuses specifically on emerging and mid-career artists. Its exhibition program rotates regularly across painting, original prints, and sculpture, with a curatorial approach that sits closer to a museum than a commercial showroom. For visitors who want to see what is happening right now in American contemporary art, rather than what established names are producing, Momentum is worth dedicated time.

The Woolworth Walk on Haywood Street occupies the former F. W. Woolworth building downtown and now houses over 160 local artists across multiple floors. It is the kind of place that local visitors tend to discover by accident and then return to deliberately. The range of work on display, from photography to fiber arts to ceramics to painting, reflects the breadth of Asheville's studio community more than any single gallery can. The building's history adds a layer of resonance: Woolworth lunch counters were among the sites of civil rights sit-ins across the South in the 1960s, and the building in Asheville now houses a cooperative of local makers. That is a transformation with some weight to it.

West Asheville, historically the scrappier and more residential side of the city, has developed its own concentration of smaller galleries, studios, and pop-up exhibition spaces along Haywood Road. These tend to run on smaller budgets and bigger ambitions, which gives the neighborhood its particular creative energy. The work on view in West Asheville galleries often skews more experimental and less market-oriented than what you find downtown, which is part of the point.

Saturdays in Asheville have a rhythm that visitors from less art-saturated cities find slightly disorienting. Between the RAD Art Stroll on second Saturdays, the Asheville Art Museum, the Folk Art Center, and whatever is happening in half a dozen West Asheville spaces, it is genuinely possible to spend the entire day looking at art made by people who live within 20 miles of where you are standing.

The Literary Layer

The visual arts and music get most of the attention, but Asheville has a literary culture that runs alongside them and is easy to miss if you are not looking for it.

Malaprop's Bookstore and Cafe on Haywood Street has been an independent bookstore since 1982, making it one of the longest-running independent bookstores in the

South. It is the kind of place that has survived the rise of Amazon, the recession, the pandemic, and a hurricane by being deeply embedded in the community rather than simply stocking books. Its event calendar is aggressive: author readings, poetry nights, book clubs, and literary discussions run throughout the year, and it draws writers of national standing who are willing to make the trip to Asheville because the audience is reliably engaged.

Before any of this existed, the whole thing nearly didn't. In 1980, the city of Asheville announced a plan to raze 11 blocks of downtown and replace them with a shopping mall. The targeted area ran roughly from Broadway west to Rankin Avenue, College Street north to Interstate 240, which is to say the entire North Lexington Avenue corridor that now defines the city's independent business and arts district. The developer was a Philadelphia firm called Strouse, Greenberg and Company. The price tag was a $40 million bond referendum. The Chamber of Commerce was for it. The newspaper was for it. The local television station was for it. Mission Hospital was for it. Almost every institution in the city lined up behind the idea that the future of downtown Asheville was an indoor food court and 330,000 square feet of department stores. A UNC Asheville student named Peggy Gardner organized 135 volunteers to wrap the entire proposed demolition area in cloth on a single April night in 1980, so residents could see with their own eyes what was about to disappear. Kathryn Long, who owned a shop on North Lexington Avenue, and her brother-in-law Wayne Caldwell founded Save Downtown Asheville and spent two years attending every city council meeting, every planning hearing, and every public forum they could find. In November 1981, voters defeated the bond referendum two to one. The mall was never built. The buildings that would have been rubble are the buildings you are walking through now.

The bookstore, the music venue, the drum circle, the benches in Pritchard Park: very little of what defines downtown Asheville today got there on its own. Julian Price arrived in 1989 from California, heir to a family fortune, and chose downtown Asheville at a moment when downtown Asheville was mostly a case study in municipal neglect. He founded Public Interest Projects with Pat Whalen the following year, invested more than $15 million in buildings and businesses, and made a deliberate decision to keep his name off everything he touched. He thought a downtown needed a bookstore, so Malaprop's exists. He thought it needed a serious music venue, so the Orange Peel exists. He put money behind restaurants, civic spaces, the Urban Trail, the Mountain Xpress, and the benches in Pritchard Park where the drum circle happens every Friday. The International Downtown Association gave him their highest award for Placemaking. He died in 2001. Most people drinking a beer at the Orange Peel have no idea who he was, which is exactly what he wanted.

The literary scene around Malaprop's includes a working community of novelists, poets, memoirists, and essayists who have made Asheville their home. The mountains have attracted writers for generations, partly for the isolation and partly for the landscape, but the current concentration is also a function of the same creative gravity that pulls visual artists.

Thomas Wolfe grew up in Asheville and described the city in *Look Homeward, Angel* in terms that made his neighbors furious and made the city famous. The novel was banned from the Asheville public library for years after its 1929 publication. His mother's boardinghouse on North Market Street, the real-life model for the novel's Dixieland, is now a state historic site and National Historic Landmark. The relationship between Asheville and writers has had complicated moments, but it has never stopped.

The Southern Appalachian Writers Cooperative, Story Parlor, and various other organizations support working writers with readings, workshops, and publication opportunities. The literary scene is not as visible as the visual arts, in part because writers tend to work in private. But it is present, and it is one more thread in the fabric of a city that treats the making of things, whether pots or paintings or paragraphs, as legitimate work.

Asheville does not merely have festivals. It builds cultural ecosystems around them and then continues operating those ecosystems year-round.

LEAF, the Lake Eden Arts Festival, was founded in 1995 by Jennifer Pickering at a former summer camp on Lake Eden in nearby Black Mountain. Pickering resisted the label of music festival from the start. LEAF is, in her framing, a world-traveling community that camps together for a weekend, where genres do not compete and healing arts and poetry share the schedule with musicians from West Africa, the Caribbean, and the American South. In 2025, LEAF celebrated its 30th anniversary, drawing 6,000 attendees and headliners from Benin and Ghana after the 2024 festival was canceled by Helene.

For its 2026 festival, scheduled for October 16 through 18, LEAF is moving. Pickering, who owned the Lake Eden property, stepped down as executive director at the end of 2025, and the festival is relocating to Deerfields, a 940-acre family property in Mills River about 30 minutes from Asheville that adjoins Pisgah National Forest. LEAF has been candid that it is at a financial crossroads, saying the 2026 festival could be its last if community support does not come through. For a 30-year-old institution that has outlasted floods, a pandemic, and the departure of its founder, that is a statement worth taking seriously.

Bob Moog, inventor of the synthesizer that bears his name, moved to Asheville in 1978 after falling in love with the mountains during a stay at the Grove Park Inn and lived here for the last 27 years of his life. He embodied the Asheville archetype exactly: a brilliant, unconventional thinker doing highly specialized work far from any traditional center of industry. The fact that the defining pioneer of electronic synthesized music made his home in a city known for hand-thrown pottery and Appalachian woodturning is, in retrospect, completely predictable.

For years, outsiders thought Moog's legacy here was just a tourist attraction. Moogfest ran from 2010 to 2015, drawing thousands downtown and turning a music festival into a cultural symposium, before relocating to Durham and dying out in 2019. The factory store and public tours at 160 Broadway Street ran for 13 years as a pilgrimage site for synth fans. Then the Broadway storefront closed in late June 2024. As of early 2026, the property has been sold and occupied by another business entirely.

Asheville did not panic. The festival left and the retail storefront closed because Asheville does not care about fleeting spectacles. Moog's engineering and instrument construction continue quietly in the area, the work having retreated from the public eye without fanfare. The Bob Moog Foundation remains in the city to fund music education and synthesizer research. The Moogseum anchors his legacy downtown. The durable infrastructure stayed. If the absence of a tourist gift shop disappoints you, that is useful information about whether you and this city are compatible.

The Asheville Fringe Arts Festival, now in its 24th year, was founded in 2002 and grew from a single venue to a week-long multi-venue event. When it bleeds out of the theaters and onto the pavement, you are not going to encounter a guy with a poorly tuned acoustic guitar. You are going to navigate a gauntlet that its own organizers describe as featuring "queer clowns and killer banjos." The festival gives 50% of ticket revenue directly back to performing artists, which is an unusual commitment for any arts organization, and one that keeps the talent both local and unapologetically strange.

The City That Also Has the Largest Private Home in America

Here is something Asheville manages to do that most cities cannot: it holds wildly contradictory things simultaneously and nobody seems particularly bothered.

The Biltmore Estate sits about three miles from Firestorm Books and Coffee. The Biltmore is a 250-room French Renaissance chateau on 8,000 acres, commissioned by George Vanderbilt and completed in 1895. It is the largest privately owned home ever built in the United States, a monument to Gilded Age ambition on a scale that makes other monuments to Gilded Age ambition look modest. Vanderbilt hired Richard Morris Hunt, the first American architect to train at the Ecole des Beaux-Arts in Paris, to design the house, and brought Frederick Law Olmsted, the landscape architect behind Central Park, to design the grounds. He assembled a library of 22,000 volumes, collected art from multiple continents, and installed an indoor swimming pool, a bowling alley, a banquet hall that seats 64 under a 70-foot ceiling, and a conservatory that required its own staff.

It employs thousands of people, hosts well over a million visitors a year, and operates a winery producing award-winning wines from grapes grown on the estate. By any measure it is one of the most significant tourist attractions in the American Southeast, and calling it merely a house is technically accurate in the way that calling the Atlantic Ocean merely a puddle is technically accurate.

Firestorm Books and Coffee has operated since 2008 as a worker-owned, collectively self-managed radical bookstore and community event space in West Asheville. It carries titles from anarchist publishers like AK Press and PM Press, serves vegan pastries, hosts film screenings and trans writing circles and prison books packaging parties, and is exactly what it sounds like in the most unironic possible way. Its operating model is the institutional opposite of the Biltmore in every respect: no hierarchy, no investors, no gift shop with monogrammed bathrobes.

Three miles apart. Both thriving. The city holds a 250-room French Renaissance chateau with an indoor swimming pool and a worker-owned collective that hosts trans writing circles and prison books packaging parties in the same breath and does not appear to notice the distance.

That coexistence is not charming local color. It is a genuine condition of living here, and it is worth being honest about. Outsiders tend to move to cities wanting a cohesive neighborhood identity, a legible set of values they can orient themselves around. Asheville offers no such comfort. The city is not organized around the idea that one thing must defeat another, which means you will find zero ideological comfort zones. The Biltmore and Firestorm, the synthesizer museum and the 30-year-old world music festival at a financial crossroads, the queer-led congregation and one of the most conservative land holdings in the region: all of it coexists without resolution. If you need your neighbors to make sense, you will lose your mind here.

The Biltmore is genuinely worth seeing. The house is extraordinary by any architectural measure, the grounds are legitimately beautiful, and the winery produces wines that have earned real recognition. None of this, however, has made it universally beloved by the people who live three miles away. Adult admission runs between $78 and

$132 depending on the season, which is the kind of price point that turns a casual afternoon into a considered decision. Many Asheville residents will tell you they have never been inside, with a tone that suggests they are not especially bothered by this. The Biltmore draws its own enormous audience from elsewhere, and locals hav generally made peace with the arrangement: you go do your thing over there, and we will do ours over here.

Most cities resolve their contradictions. Asheville seems to prefer collecting them. It is possible that nobody here has noticed, or possible that everyone has noticed and simply does not consider it a problem requiring a solution.

The Queer Capital of the Mountains

Asheville is the most LGBTQ-dense city in North Carolina, and it is not a close competition. The Asheville metro area has 83% more LGBTQ-identified residents than the typical American city or town. Buncombe County has 15.5 same-sex couples per 1,000 residents; the city of Asheville itself has 19.7 per 1,000, the highest rate of any city in the state, well ahead of Charlotte, Raleigh, Durham, and Chapel Hill. The Advocate named Asheville one of the Gayest Cities in America in 2012. In 2020, the Human Rights Campaign gave the city a perfect score on its Municipal Equality Index.

What makes Asheville's queer culture distinct is not the existence of a gay neighborhood, because there isn't one in the conventional sense. There is no Castro, no Boystown, no clearly delineated district. Instead, queer life runs through the entire city. O.Henry's, one of the oldest gay bars in North Carolina, sits downtown alongside Scandals, which runs drag shows Thursday through Sunday. The integration is the point: queer culture in Asheville is not confined to a neighborhood; it is distributed throughout the fabric of the city.

The Blue Ridge Pride Festival, founded in 2009, drew 2,000 people to its inaugural gathering. It now brings between 10,000 and 14,000 people annually to Pack Square Park in September, with 200 vendors, music on two stages, and an evening drag showcase. CNN has named it one of the world's best places to celebrate Pride. A Pride festival that draws that kind of attendance to a city of 95,000 is not a niche event. It is a civic institution.

The organizations supporting queer life in Asheville extend well beyond the festival. Youth OUTright serves queer youth ages 11 through 24. Tranzmission has been providing education and support for transgender and non-binary people since 2001. PFLAG Asheville, founded in 2018, offers community resources and support. Mountain Spirit MCC, a queer-led congregation, holds Sunday worship explicitly rooted in queer perspectives and wisdom.

The welcoming congregations movement in Asheville has also produced something worth noting. Mars Hill United Methodist Church, a reconciling congregation, participated in the Blue Ridge Pride welcoming procession, describing their position in the simplest possible terms: they welcome and celebrate every child of God without exception.

The geography of tolerance in Asheville extends into institutions that sometimes represent the reverse of it elsewhere. In a state that has had a complicated legislative history with LGBTQ rights, Asheville represents a genuinely different set of local norms, backed by local ordinance and expressed in the daily texture of the city.

The Town Down the Road and the College That Changed Everything

The college is long gone, but the town of Black Mountain carries the legacy better than any historical marker could. Its walkable downtown is dense with independent shops, working studios, and restaurants, and the surrounding community has quietly accumulated a serious concentration of working artists and musicians who chose proximity to the college's ghost over the noise of the city. The lakeside camp that hosts LEAF sits in its orbit. For people who want the cultural density of the Asheville region without the full weight of a small city, Black Mountain is worth serious consideration.

The broader Western North Carolina region has a long-established relationship with studio craft that Black Mountain College amplified rather than created. Potters, weavers, and woodworkers have worked in these mountains since before the college existed. The clay body of the Southern Appalachians has particular properties that attracted studio potters; the forest traditions of the region produced furniture makers and carvers whose work predates the arts and crafts movement. What Black Mountain College did was give that regional tradition an international frame, connecting the Appalachian craft lineage to European modernism and to the wider currents of 20th century art.

That combination, deep regional craft tradition meeting the most advanced international art thinking of the mid-20th century, is unusual. Most art communities have one or the other. Very few have both. Asheville still benefits from the tension between them, and you can see it most clearly in the RAD, where a woodturner making vessels from locally salvaged timber might have a studio two doors down from a painter working in a tradition that runs through Rauschenberg and the New York School.

Why Any of This Matters If You Are Considering a Move

Culture is easy to undervalue when evaluating a potential home. You count the schools, the commute times, the grocery stores, the hospital quality. You look at the crime statistics and the tax rates and the real estate inventory. Culture goes in the soft category, the nice-to-have column.

Asheville makes a case for reconsidering that framework.

The creative economy here is not a supplement to the real economy. It is load-bearing. The arts draw the tourists who fill the hotels and restaurants. The cultural identity of the city attracts the remote workers and transplants who have driven the real estate market. The festivals and galleries and studios and drum circles give residents reasons to stay and give visitors reasons to come back. Take away the arts infrastructure and you do not have a smaller version of the same city. You have a different city.

More than that, the density of creative culture means that living here, even if you have no professional connection to the arts, means being in close proximity to people who make things, think unconventionally, and have made peace with the idea that the rules are more flexible than advertised. That proximity has effects on a community that are difficult to quantify but easy to feel. Cities where creative people concentrate tend to produce more interesting conversations, more experimental restaurants, more unexpected public spaces, and a general tolerance for novelty that makes daily life a little less predictable in the good sense.

There is also something to be said for living in a place that knows what it is. Asheville has been refining its identity for decades. It did not become weird by accident or by marketing. It became weird because the people who were drawn to it kept arriving with the same disposition, the same appetite for a place where the standard scripts did not apply, and they built institutions around that disposition.

The college, the arts district, the festivals, the LGBTQ community organizations, the bookstore, the drum circle:

all of it is the accumulated expression of people who chose this particular mountain city because they wanted something that most cities were not offering.

That accumulated expression has practical consequences. Cities with strong creative identities tend to generate a certain kind of social permission, an unspoken agreement that you are not required to live exactly like everyone else. The couple who decides to open a ceramics studio instead of pursuing more sensible careers finds more community support here than in most places.

The retiree who wants to learn glassblowing or join a choral group or start painting at 65 finds the infrastructure already in place. The family that moved from somewhere more conventional and has not entirely figured out where they fit yet tends to discover, in Asheville, that not entirely figuring it out is considered a reasonable and even admirable position.

If you are the kind of person who has always found the pressure to fit in slightly exhausting, Asheville will feel like a relief. The city has organized itself, deliberately and over a long period of time, around the idea that the weird stuff is not the problem to be solved. It is the foundation everything else is built on.

The restaurants, the breweries, the mountain views, the hiking, the architecture, the real estate: all of it works precisely because the weird already owns the neighborhood.

Don't move here if you want to fit in. You won't. You'll fit somewhere entirely different instead, and after a few months, you probably won't miss fitting in at all.

CHAPTER NINE

DON'T MOVE HERE
IF YOU THINK
SMALL TOWNS STAY SMALL

Asheville has a reputation problem. Not the kind where people think badly of it, but the opposite kind, where people carry around a mental image of the place that stopped updating sometime around 2010. They picture a quirky little mountain city with a good craft beer scene, some interesting restaurants, and a charming downtown where you can walk to everything in twenty minutes. That picture is not wrong, exactly. It's just about fifteen years out of date.

The Asheville that exists today is something more complicated and, depending on your priorities, either more appealing or more alarming than the postcard version. It is a city in the middle of becoming something, without being entirely sure yet what that something is. That uncertainty, as it turns out, is part of what makes it worth paying attention to.

Most cities know what they are. They settled into an identity decades ago and have been managing it ever since, polishing the parts that attract visitors and quietly ignoring the rest. Asheville hasn't finished that process. It's still in negotiation with itself about what kind of place it wants to be, what it owes to the people who built it, and what it should ask of the people arriving now. That negotiation is occasionally uncomfortable to watch. It is also honest in a way that more settled cities rarely manage.

The Numbers Don't Lie, Even When They're Inconvenient

Start with population, because population is where you see the shape of a place's future most clearly. The city of Asheville itself has grown from around 69,000 people at the turn of the century to roughly 95,000 today. That's a meaningful jump for a city this size, but it understates what's actually happening. The Asheville metropolitan statistical area, which takes in Buncombe, Haywood, Henderson, and Madison counties, held around 369,000 people in 2000 and has grown to more than 422,000. That's not a small town getting a little bigger. That's a regional economy reaching critical mass.

The distinction between the city and the MSA matters more here than it does in most places. Asheville proper is surrounded by terrain that limits how it can expand. You can't sprawl outward the way a Sunbelt city does, because the mountains are in the way. Growth spills into surrounding communities: Weaverville, Black Mountain, Swannanoa, Arden, pockets of Buncombe County that have their own character and their own complicated feelings about what's happening around them. The result is a metropolitan area considerably larger than the city at its center, and that mismatch shapes everything from traffic patterns to housing supply to the way local politics works.

Population growth is abstract until you connect it to jobs. Since 2010, the Asheville MSA has added tens of thousands of jobs and more than 50,000 people. Fifteen years ago, Asheville was a quirky mountain city with a good music scene and some unusually serious restaurants. Somewhere between then and now it became a regional economy, and the city is still figuring out what that means for the people who were here first.

These are not glamorous tech-sector announcements.

They're healthcare jobs, education jobs, construction and trades jobs, and the full supporting cast of a regional economy trying to grow up fast. The mix matters. A region that grows primarily on tourism and hospitality is a region with a structurally fragile employment base, one that Helene exposed with considerable clarity. Diversification into healthcare, manufacturing, and education creates a foundation less susceptible to a single bad quarter, a single storm, a single shift in visitor behavior.

To understand what 422,000 people actually means, it helps to think about what it doesn't mean. It doesn't mean 422,000 people living inside city limits. It means 422,000 people whose economic center of gravity is Asheville, working there, shopping there, relying on its hospitals and highways and airport, even when they go home to a county with a different name. That distinction matters because it tells you something important about the pressure the city is absorbing on behalf of a population much larger than its own tax base was designed to support.

The gap between the city proper and the MSA has been widening for two decades, and it will keep widening. The surrounding counties have grown faster in percentage terms because they offer what the core increasingly cannot: land that can actually be built on, at a price that doesn't drequire a second mortgage on your retirement account. Henderson County to the south, Haywood County to the west, Madison County to the north: the communities that people moved to specifically to avoid becoming Asheville are becoming Asheville. The mountains didn't protect them. The distance didn't protect them. The price difference is protecting them for now. Now is getting shorter.

Growth projections for the broader Asheville region suggest continued expansion through 2030 and beyond, with some estimates placing the increase at roughly four percent over five years and closer to eight or nine percent over ten. The arithmetic is worth sitting with for a moment. Even a modest percentage of 422,000 represents tens of thousands of additional people, in a geography with finite room for them. You cannot add that many people to a landscape this constrained without fundamentally reshaping what it looks like and how it functions. The question is not whether the reshaping will happen. It is whether anyone is steering it.

Most of the time, growth decides for itself. That is the honest answer, even in cities with excellent planning departments. Planners can shape the conditions under which development happens, can incentivize one outcome over another, can draw lines on maps that encourage density here and discourage it there. But they cannot override the fundamental math of supply and demand operating in a landscape where buildable land is genuinely finite. When more people want to be in a place than that place can accommodate, the excess goes somewhere. In Asheville's case, somewhere is increasingly everywhere else in the region.

The AVL 5x5 Strategy and What It Actually Means

The Asheville Area Chamber of Commerce would like you to know that it is not simply hoping growth happens. It has a plan. The plan has a name: AVL 5x5. The name comes from five industry focus areas and a five-year horizon, now in its fourth cycle targeting 2030. Someone in a conference room came up with that framework, presented it on slides, and the region adopted it, which is exactly what regions do when they want to feel like they're steering the ship rather than clinging to the railing.

The strategy's signature achievement is a target wage: $60,886. That is the average annual salary across newly announced jobs in the most recent cycle, a figure the Economic Development Coalition has declared represents what a household needs to cover basic expenses in the Asheville MSA without chronic financial stress. The Chamber of Commerce is using this number as a benchmark. Which means a regional business organization is now running on a spreadsheet that tells employers what to pay. Progress.

The reason the Chamber had to invent a wage target is not complicated. Asheville spent two decades building a reputation as a destination, and that reputation generated jobs, and those jobs, on average, did not pay enough to live where the people holding them were expected to show up for work. The server at the restaurant that gets written up in national food magazines cannot afford the city where the restaurant operates. The chamber discovered this, convened some committees, and produced a document. The document is a genuine improvement over no document. That is the most honest way to put it.

The current plan includes something called "advanced manufacturing," which is where things get genuinely interesting, because "advanced manufacturing" is the economic development phrase that regions deploy when they want to sound like the future without specifying what they mean. In Asheville's case it means, among other things, GE Aviation, which has expanded its regional facility through successive plan cycles and produces components for aircraft engines. Yes. Aircraft engines. In the city famous for street musicians and pickle-brined chicken sandwiches. The plan is not incoherent. The region actually has a manufacturing heritage, and the creative economy turns out to be weirdly compatible with precision production. Whether that compatibility survives the gap between the slides and the shop floor is a question that will take another five-year cycle or two to fully answer.

What Growing Up Costs

Growth doesn't come free, and Asheville is paying for it in ways visible from every angle. The housing market tells the most direct story, and we've already told it: prices have more than doubled since the early 2010s, a run of appreciation so steep that it reshapes not just what people can buy but who can afford to stay. That story belongs to Chapter 3. What belongs here is what comes next.

The housing supply problem is not something a good economy fixes on its own. The city has set a goal of adding 14,000 new homes over 25 years to keep pace with projected population growth through 2050. To hit that, Asheville needs to build 560 units every single year. In recent years, it hasn't come close.

A $20 million affordable housing bond passed in November 2024, and the city is deploying those funds through its Housing Trust Fund and the WNC Affordable Housing Loan Fund, which was created in early 2024 through a partnership between Self-Help Credit Union and Dogwood Health Trust. These are real commitments. Whether they're sufficient commitments is a harder question, and the city's planners would probably be the first to admit it.

Where Do Tens of Thousands of People Go When the Mountains Don't Move?

More people are coming whether Asheville is ready or not. Regional projections suggest the MSA could add somewhere between 30,000 and 40,000 residents over the next decade, comparable to the current population of Buncombe County outside the city limits. Imagine adding that many people in ten years, in a landscape where the mountains have already decided how many roads there are.

The question of where those people physically go is one

that Asheville's planners are trying to answer honestly, and the honest answer is complicated in ways that most growing cities don't have to face. The terrain is not a metaphor. The Blue Ridge and the Black Mountains and the Pisgah National Forest don't negotiate. They don't rezone. A city in the Piedmont with a booming population can expand its footprint in any direction without encountering anything more resistant than political will and soybean fields. Asheville doesn't have that option. Developable land within reasonable commuting distance of downtown is finite in ways that are visible on any topographic map, and that constraint doesn't ease as the population grows. It tightens.

The communities currently sitting at the edges of the metro area — places like Weaverville to the north, Black Mountain to the east, Swannanoa and Canton to the west — are likely to absorb a disproportionate share of the incoming population precisely because they offer what the core city increasingly cannot: available land, lower prices, and in some cases higher elevation. That absorption will transform those communities in ways their current residents may not have signed up for. The small-town character that made them attractive satellites of Asheville tends not to survive rapid growth intact.

What emerges from all of this, if the projections hold, is a metropolitan area that looks less like a city with surrounding towns and more like a continuous developed landscape threading through the mountain valleys, interrupted by terrain too steep to build on. The Asheville of 2035 may be recognizable in its cultural identity and its civic institutions while being almost unrecognizable in its physical footprint. The place survived and in many ways flourished through the last major transformation. But the pace of the next decade's growth, combined with geographic constraints that have no policy solution, means the question of where the next wave of residents fits is not one that planning documents alone can answer.

There's also the commute problem, which the data obscure but residents feel every day. When growth pushes people into satellite communities to find housing they can afford, the drive back into the city follows routes that the terrain had already constrained before the population was this size. The corridor north into Weaverville runs through a single meaningful highway. The route east to Black Mountain runs through a mountain pass. The options west toward Canton are limited by geography in ways that a bypass can improve but not eliminate. The transportation infrastructure required to move a regional population of this size through mountain terrain is genuinely difficult to build, genuinely expensive to maintain, and genuinely inadequate at present peak hours in ways that anyone who has tried to get somewhere at five o'clock on a Friday afternoon already knows. The rail conversation exists, in part, because roads in this landscape have a hard ceiling that the population does not.

The mountains will have something to say about all of it. They always do.

What Happens to the Towns That Didn't Ask to Be Suburbs

Let's talk about Weaverville, because Weaverville is where you can watch this process happening in real time at a scale that's still comprehensible as a human story rather than a demographic abstraction. The town sits about eight miles north of downtown Asheville on a ridge above the French Broad valley. Its entire commercial district occupies about four blocks. On a Tuesday afternoon in October, you can find a parking spot without praying about it. It has the feeling of a town that knows what it is and has arranged itself accordingly.

That feeling is increasingly at odds with what the real estate market is doing. Home prices in Weaverville have risen sharply as buyers priced out of Buncombe County's core look north for options that don't require choosing between housing and everything else. The buyers arriving now are not moving to Weaverville. They're moving to Asheville and happen to be living in Weaverville. That distinction, small as it sounds, reshapes the way a town functions. It changes who's in the coffee shop on a weekday morning, what political concerns dominate the town council agenda, and what a local business owner can charge for a sandwich without losing half the lunch crowd.

Weaverville's growth challenge is compounded by its geography. The town sits at the end of a single meaningful corridor, US-19/23, which runs south into Asheville, and that same road carries every commuter coming down from Madison County and the northern valleys. There is no alternate route that meaningfully shortcuts the distance. When that highway backs up, which it does with increasing frequency during morning and evening peaks, the backup extends north through Weaverville itself. The town didn't generate that traffic. It is simply in the way of it.

Black Mountain is a different story, though the ending looks similar from a distance. It sits about fifteen miles east of downtown Asheville on the far side of the Swannanoa valley, tucked against the base of the Blue Ridge escarpment in a way that gives it both dramatic scenery and a slightly elevated position relative to the valley floor. The town has had a serious arts identity for decades, and that identity made it attractive to a certain kind of buyer long before the rest of the region started looking east for affordability.

The problem Black Mountain faces is not that people have discovered it. People discovered it years ago. The problem is the volume. There's a meaningful difference between a town that attracts a steady trickle of buyers who genuinely want to be there and a town that absorbs a surge of buyers who want to be somewhere nearby and have settled for the closest affordable option. The first group tends to invest in the community. The second group tends to commute through it. Black Mountain is now getting both simultaneously, and the two populations have different relationships to the place they're living in.

Its access to Asheville runs through the Swannanoa valley on I-40, which is one of the few stretches of interstate in the region but shares a single corridor with freight traffic coming over the mountain from Tennessee. When that route slows, through accidents, winter weather, or sheer volume, the alternatives involve going over the mountain rather than through it, which is not a sentence that makes most commuters feel better about their life choices. Black Mountain's charm survives the drive. Whether that trade-off remains acceptable as the volume increases is something every new resident is quietly running the math on.

Swannanoa sits between Black Mountain and Asheville proper, running along the river that shares its name through a narrow valley that left it historically industrial and perpetually undervalued compared to its neighbors. It was the kind of place that offered proximity to Asheville at a price that reflected its lack of cachet, and for a long time that was a workable arrangement for buyers who prioritized location over prestige. Then Helene came through the Swannanoa valley with a force that nobody in the region had experienced in living memory, and that arrangement changed overnight.

The storm drew a line through Swannanoa that its recovery has not erased. Properties at lower elevations in the flood path are selling slowly if they're selling at all, with insurance questions that don't have clean answers and repair costs that exceed what the pre-flood market could justify. Properties on higher ground above the flood line are being competed over by buyers who understand exactly what they're paying for: the same mountain proximity and relative affordability, plus the demonstrated knowledge that the ground under them stayed dry when everything else didn't. It's a bifurcated market inside a single small community, and navigating it requires local knowledge that no online listing can fully provide.

Canton is the most complicated piece of this picture, and the one that gets the least attention in conversations about Asheville's growth. It sits further west on the Pigeon River, in Haywood County, which puts it just outside the Buncombe County core but well within the economic pull of the Asheville MSA. For most of the twentieth century Canton was a mill town, organized around the Champion International mill, later the Pactiv Evergreen mill, the way a major employer always organizes a small town. When that mill closed in 2023 after more than a century of operation, it left a hole that's visible in the local economy and in the faces of people who had structured their working lives around its continued existence.

What makes Canton's situation genuinely interesting, and genuinely uncertain, is that it's navigating post-industrial identity loss at the same moment the Asheville growth wave is arriving at its doorstep. The housing stock is older and more affordable than the regional average. The community has a working-class character that hasn't yet been polished into the kind of curated authenticity that drives up property values in places like Black Mountain. That combination, cheap and real, is exactly what a certain kind of buyer is looking for as the price of admission to the rest of the metro area climbs past what they were expecting to spend.

Canton didn't have to go looking for its next chapter. The next chapter showed up at the county line and started moving in.

None of this is unique to Asheville. But the speed of it is accelerating, and the buffer that geography once provided, the sense that a town could stay a town because the mountains between it and the city were inconvenient enough to limit exposure, is eroding faster than most of these communities had anticipated. Inconvenient is not the same as inaccessible, and in a region where the core has priced out a growing share of its own workforce, inconvenient starts to look like a reasonable trade. Ask anyone driving forty minutes each way on US-19/23 whether the commute is worth it. Most of them will say yes, at least for now. Come back in five years and ask again.

What Helene Told the Real Estate Market

Tropical Storm Helene made landfall in September 2024 and caused an estimated \$78.7 billion in damage, making it the seventh-costliest Atlantic hurricane on record. The storm disrupted water service for weeks, damaged thousands of homes and businesses, and sent shockwaves through the regional economy. But for the purposes of understanding where Asheville grows next, the most consequential thing Helene did wasn't the destruction. It was the information.

Helene was not, technically speaking, a hurricane when it reached Western North Carolina. It had weakened to a tropical storm by then, which is one of those meteorological details that feels darkly funny in retrospect, because what arrived in the French Broad River valley behaved nothing like what most people picture when they hear 'tropical storm.' Rainfall totals across the Southern Appalachians were so extreme that some measuring stations recorded precipitation levels with a statistical recurrence interval of more than a thousand years. The rivers didn't flood. They became something else entirely. And in doing so, they drew a line on the regional map that no zoning board had put there, dividing the landscape into places that flooded and places that didn't.

That line is now part of every serious real estate conversation in the Asheville region.

Elevation in Western North Carolina is no longer just an aesthetic preference. It's a climate calculation. The floods of Helene followed the rivers, the valleys, the low-lying industrial corridors that were built near water because that's where industry has always gone. The neighborhoods that sat higher on the ridge lines came through the storm in substantially better shape than the ones closer to the French Broad and the Swannanoa. That distinction is now baked into buyer psychology in ways it wasn't before September 2024, and it is reshaping where people want to purchase, what they'll pay for the privilege, and consequently what the regional growth footprint looks like going forward.

The demographic group doing the most aggressive climate-motivated calculation tends to be older, wealthier, and mobile. These are remote workers in their fifties and early sixties, retirees with meaningful assets, people who have done the math on where they want to spend the next twenty years and concluded that a temperate climate, access to good healthcare, and a relatively low probability of catastrophic weather events is worth a significant premium. Asheville checks most of those boxes. The elevation premium that Helene made explicit is, for this group, a feature rather than a bug. They want to be above the flood line. They can afford to be above the flood line. And when a population of well-capitalized buyers competes specifically for the higher-ground properties that the rest of the market has also identified as more desirable and more resilient, the price pressure on exactly those properties becomes intense in ways that cascade through the entire regional housing market.

This dynamic has a name in urban economics, though not a flattering one. Climate gentrification is the process by which higher-elevation or otherwise climate-resilient real estate becomes increasingly valuable as climate risk becomes more legible to the broader market. Miami researchers documented it happening in that city along elevation lines years before Helene made the concept vivid in the Southern Appalachians. In Asheville's case, the effect is amplified by the fact that the most climate-resilient land is also, by definition, the most topographically constrained. There isn't an unlimited supply of ridge-line property within twenty minutes of downtown. There is an increasing supply of buyers who have specifically identified that property as where they want to be.

What makes the Asheville version of this phenomenon worth understanding in some detail is the speed at which it happened. In Miami, climate gentrification developed over years as sea-level projections gradually worked their way into the consciousness of buyers and their real estate agents. In Western North Carolina, it happened in a single weekend in September 2024. Helene didn't gradually shift buyer psychology. It replaced one psychology with another, almost overnight. Before the storm, elevation was a preference. After it, elevation was a credential.

The buyers doing the most aggressive elevation-driven purchasing tend to arrive already knowing what they want. They've looked at topographic maps. They've cross-referenced FEMA flood zones with the neighborhood boundaries visible in Helene damage reports. Some of them have hired consultants. This is not an exaggeration. There is a small but growing industry of climate relocation advisors who work specifically with high-net-worth clients to identify properties that optimize for resilience across a range of climate scenarios. Asheville was already on their radar before Helene. After it, the region moved up several places on the list.

The mechanics of how this translates into housing prices are worth understanding, because the effects are not limited to the ridge-line properties that buyers are explicitly targeting. When well-capitalized buyers compete intensely for a specific subset of properties, they push prices up in that subset. That creates a new price ceiling in that tier of the market, which in turn pushes buyers who can't meet it into the next tier down, which pushes prices up there too. The elevation premium propagates downward through the market, raising prices on properties that have no particular climate advantage, simply because the buyers who would have settled for those properties have been priced out of the tier above them.

The people absorbing the cost of this cascade are, predictably, the people with the fewest options. Longtime Asheville residents who rent, who are trying to buy their first home, who work in the service and hospitality sectors that keep the city running: these are the households for whom the elevation premium is not a strategy but a problem. They cannot afford to optimize for climate resilience. They need to afford a place to live, and the price floor in the parts of the market accessible to them keeps rising in response to pressures they have no way to control. You can understand why every individual buyer is making a rational decision and still recognize that the aggregate outcome is a city that is quietly sorting itself by wealth along topographic lines.

There's a historical irony buried in this that's worth naming. Asheville's low-lying industrial corridors, the neighborhoods and commercial strips that sit along the French Broad and the Swannanoa, were built where they were because water was an industrial resource, not a threat. The people who worked in those industries often lived nearby, in modest housing that was affordable precisely because it occupied terrain nobody with more options would have chosen. For a long time, low ground was where working people lived. Helene didn't change that relationship so much as make it catastrophically visible. What climate gentrification does, in the aftermath, is price the survivors of that catastrophe off the higher ground too.

Building the Infrastructure a Regional City Requires

Growing into a regional city requires more than housing. It requires the unglamorous machinery of civic investment: bonds and budgets and planning documents and wage targets. Most people find this deeply boring right up until the moment they don't. Asheville is in the middle of building all of that machinery, with varying degrees of confidence and competence, and the scale of it is worth understanding because it tells you something about how seriously the city is taking its own growth.

Here is something that doesn't get said enough about Asheville: the voters. In November 2024, weeks after Helene, with the city still in active emergency response and water service only recently restored to most neighborhoods, Asheville residents went to the polls and approved an $80 million general obligation bond package split across four categories: affordable housing, transportation, parks and recreation, and public safety. Not a modest little measure. Eighty million dollars in new debt, voted yes on by people who had just watched their city flood. That is a city telling itself, in the only language that fully counts, that it intends to still be here in twenty years and would like to be somewhat better prepared for what that involves.

The $20 million affordable housing slice of that package is a different kind of test than the rest. General obligation bonds for parks and transportation are easy yeses. A category specifically earmarked for affordable housing is where civic virtue meets neighborhood self-interest and things get complicated. People who support affordable housing in the abstract tend to have very specific feelings about the block it goes on. Approving all four categories in the same election, in the same week Asheville was still piecing itself back together, suggests a city that had gotten past the comfortable fiction that growth could be managed without deliberately deciding who gets to stay.

The $20 million is being deployed through several channels: the city's Housing Trust Fund and the WNC Affordable Housing Loan Fund, administered through Self-Help Credit Union, which will leverage city funds to enable gap financing for affordable multifamily projects. That is the theory, anyway. The practice depends on land costs, construction costs, and the willingness of lenders and developers to participate in a program that requires accepting lower returns than the open market would deliver. All three of those conditions are harder to meet in Asheville's current market than they were five years ago.

The $55 Million Baseball Problem

While the city was tallying bonds and budgets, it was also reckoning with a problem that had nothing to do with flood mitigation or affordable housing and everything to do with clubhouses. McCormick Field, renamed HomeTrust Park in April, 2026, opened in 1924. It is the third-oldest active minor league ballpark in the country, home to the Asheville Tourists and their High-A affiliation with the Houston Astros. It is also a ballpark that was not up to standard. Major League Baseball issued a facilities directive in 2021 requiring all affiliated minor league parks to meet new professional development standards. McCormick Field did not meet them. The city, which owns the stadium, had a choice: renovate or lose the team. Renovating, it turned out, would cost $38.5 million in construction, rising to $55.6 million once you factored in the life of the debt service. The city approved it anyway. This is the unglamorous machinery of civic investment in action.

The renovation is the largest single construction project in the city's history, which is a sentence worth sitting with. Not a water infrastructure overhaul. Not a school. A baseball stadium. The Buncombe County Tourism Development Authority contributed $23 million, the city $18.5 million, and Buncombe County another $5 million, with the Tourists ownership adding roughly $10.4 million, including a million dollars specifically for a new video board. The video board is very important. Groundbreaking happened in September 2024. Construction ran concurrently with the 2025 season, which means fans paid to watch a game while also watching a crane, which is a metaphor for something but it's hard to say exactly what.

The traffic situation on game nights deserves its own paragraph. McCormick Field sits on Buchanan Place, tucked against a hillside off Biltmore Avenue, in a neighborhood that was not designed for 4,000 people arriving simultaneously. The parking lot fills early. The overflow parks in the lots of nearby businesses whose owners develop complicated feelings about minor league baseball every time there's a home stand. The streets leading to the stadium run narrow and hilly in ways that seemed entirely reasonable in 1924. After a Thursday night game, the combination of outbound traffic and the city's commitment to pedestrian crosswalks produces a gridlock that suggests the planners of McCormick Field and the planners of Biltmore Avenue were working from very different assumptions about what this neighborhood would eventually become. At the council meeting where the renovation was approved, four speakers said they wanted their streets paved instead. They were not entirely wrong.

And yet. The Tourists invented Thirsty Thursday in 1983. They own the trademark. From coast to coast, minor league teams run dollar-beer promotions and call them Thirsty Thursday, and every one of them is paying tribute, consciously or not, to a promotion that started at this particular stadium in this particular mountain city. On a summer Thursday night at McCormick Field, with a dollar domestic in hand and the Blue Ridge visible beyond the outfield wall and a game playing in front of you that costs roughly nothing to attend, it is genuinely difficult to maintain a fully cynical position about the $55.6 million or the traffic on Buchanan Place or any of the rest of it. Difficult, but not impossible. The city is still paying it off in 2044.

What $60,886 Is Actually Trying to Do

The AVL 5x5 wage figure of $60,886 sounds like something a spreadsheet produced, which is fair, because it did. But what the spreadsheet was measuring is worth understanding. Asheville spent the better part of two decades building a reputation as a destination: for food, for music, for the specific combination of mountain scenery and urban culture that makes people quit their jobs in Charlotte and show up with a moving truck. That reputation generated a lot of jobs. Those jobs did not, on average, pay enough to live where the people who held them were expected to show up for work. The server who makes your dinner in a restaurant that gets written up in national magazines cannot afford to live in the city where that restaurant operates. That is the problem. $60,886 is the number someone wrote down and started trying to fix it.

$60,886 is not an arbitrary figure. The Economic Development Coalition reported it as the average annual wage across newly announced jobs in the most recent AVL 5x5 cycle, and it represents approximately what a household needs to earn in the Asheville MSA to meet basic expenses without chronic financial stress. The fact that the Chamber of Commerce is using it as a benchmark for economic development targets is itself significant. It represents a recognition from the business community that a regional economy producing a lot of low-wage jobs is not, in the long run, a healthy regional economy. Workers who can't afford to live nearby eventually stop showing up.

The current plan's focus areas include building capacity for local industries through a proposed innovation hub called the Futures Factory, attracting diversified high-wage industry, developing the entrepreneurial ecosystem through the Optimist Ventures Accelerator, catalyzing economic mobility through workforce programs, and grounding strategy in data. They reflect a deliberate attempt to grow the sectors that actually pay well rather than just the ones that are easy to grow. The regional education system is only now beginning to produce the workforce those jobs require at scale, and the gap between aspiration and reality remains honest enough to be uncomfortable.

Outdoor recreation is always part of the regional identity conversation, and always the trickiest to get right economically. The category includes everything from well-compensated product development roles at gear companies to seasonal guiding jobs that pay considerably less and come with no benefits. Asheville's identity as an outdoor destination is not in dispute. The question is whether that identity generates the kind of economic activity that fits the wage target, or whether it just generates more reasons for people to come here and spend money that flows to employers paying wages that don't. Getting this right requires recruiting the headquarters and the design studios and the R&D operations, not just more outfitters offering kayak tours to people who flew in from Atlanta.

What the Growth Skeptics Get Right

A city that doubles its metropolitan population in thirty years while its median home price does the same is a city under pressure from every direction, including from its own aspirations. The people worried about what Asheville is becoming are worried about the right things.

The satellite communities absorbing overflow growth from the Asheville core are being transformed in ways their residents didn't choose and can't easily reverse. Weaverville didn't ask to become a bedroom community for buyers priced out of Buncombe County. Black Mountain didn't campaign for the distinction of being the next affordable option in a metropolitan area where affordability is steadily retreating. These places have their own histories, their own reasons people chose them, their own civic identities that have nothing to do with being adjacent to a desirable larger city. Rapid growth tends to flatten those distinctions over time. Much of the next wave of residents will land in exactly these communities.

The climate gentrification dynamic adds a layer of pressure that's harder to see in the aggregate data but increasingly consequential at the community level. When well-capitalized buyers specifically target higher-elevation properties as climate hedges, they are making individually rational decisions that produce collectively complicated outcomes. Every ridge-line property purchased at a climate premium is one fewer option in a tier of the market that people without significant capital have historically relied upon. The elevation premium is not inherently malicious. It is, however, a mechanism for concentrating the costs of climate risk on the people least equipped to absorb them. The math is simple. The implications are not.

The investments underway are real, and they matter, but they don't close the gap between what the region is becoming and who can afford to be part of it. The passenger rail, if it gets built, will serve everyone who rides. The affordable housing bond directly addresses the households that can't compete in the open market. But $20 million against a housing market this size is less a solution than a signal of intent. The gap between intent and adequacy is where the hardest planning conversations happen, in Asheville and in every city facing the same math.

The Counterintuitive Case for Arriving Now

Here's what the growth skeptics sometimes miss. The city that exists in 2026 is a city in the middle of a genuine reinvestment cycle, coming out of a disaster that forced it to reckon with its own infrastructure in ways that a comfortable decade of rising property values had deferred. The affordable housing bond is deployed. Passenger rail is in active planning. The recovery from Helene, while incomplete, has demonstrated a community capacity for resilience that was not obvious before it was tested.

The rental market softened after Helene as some residents left and demand temporarily eased. That softening created a window that didn't exist in 2022 or 2023, when the market was running at full temperature and anything decent was gone before the listing had been live for a weekend. Home prices pulled back from their earlier peaks. The city is not cheap, and it is not going to become cheap, but there are moments in the arc of a growing city when the entry point is better than it will be in five years. This is probably one of them. Don't quote that.

The people who already live here and can't afford to stay

are running the same math and arriving at a different answer. For them, the softened market isn't an opportunity. It's the last chapter of a story that started when prices left their wages behind years ago. A good entry point for one person is someone else's exit, and in Asheville in 2026, that someone is usually a service worker, a teacher, or a musician, the exact people who made the city worth moving to in the first place.

The argument could also be made that the next storm changes everything again, that climate risk is real and that putting a city at the confluence of rivers in a mountain valley is a choice that carries consequences beyond what any amount of careful planning can fully mitigate. That argument isn't wrong. Asheville's planners are trying to build more flood resilience into infrastructure decisions going forward. But the French Broad runs where it runs, and weather systems follow their own logic regardless of what the planning documents say.

What Helene demonstrated, perhaps more than anything else, is that the civic fabric beneath the surface of this city is more durable than the surface itself. The infrastructure took damage. The institutions bent. The community held. The city has been rebuilt, imperfectly and incompletely, by the same people who built it the first time, and that continuity matters more than any single economic indicator.

For someone arriving now, there is also something less obvious to consider. A city in active recovery, with softened rents and a temporarily quieter real estate market, is a city with more social permeability than one running at full temperature. The neighbor you meet at the post-Helene neighborhood cleanup is a different kind of introduction than the one you'd have gotten at a crowded cocktail party in 2022, when the city felt like it was auditioning for a magazine cover. Recovery is not an amenity. It is, however, a context in which communities reveal what they're actually made of, and what Asheville revealed turns out to be worth knowing.

Growing Pains Are Still Growing

The most honest framing for Asheville in 2026 is this: it's a city that's too big to be a small town and not quite big enough to have fully sorted out what a big city requires. That middle space is uncomfortable. It's also where interesting things tend to happen, because the constraints that shape a mature city haven't fully calcified yet, and the people making decisions still have room to make them differently.

What's being built on top of the region's existing foundation is a layer of civic infrastructure that, when complete, will make the Asheville MSA look less like a large small town and more like a small large city. A potential train. A serious affordable housing program. An economic strategy targeting wages rather than just job counts. None of it is complete. All of it matters.

People who want a city to stay the way it was tend not to find what they're looking for when they move somewhere. Places change. The question worth asking isn't whether Asheville will stay small and charming and affordable, because it won't. The question is whether, in the process of becoming something larger, it will hold onto the things that made it worth moving to in the first place. That's a harder question, and anyone who answers it with complete confidence is guessing.

What you can say with confidence is that the people who live there are paying attention to it. They're arguing about it in town halls and county commission meetings and the comment sections of local news sites. They're passing housing bonds and designing rail corridors and building airports that treat Asheville like a destination rather than an afterthought. For a city that could easily have decided to coast on its reputation, that's quite a lot.

One Last Thing

If the title of this book fooled you for even a moment, that was the point. Every chapter was written by someone who moved to Asheville and considers that decision among the best he's ever made, which is a high bar given that it also includes marrying Joan.

My wife and I left Boston in 2008 because we were tired of winters that felt like a personal insult. We landed in Charleston, South Carolina, which solved the cold problem admirably while introducing a new one: summers so humid and relentless that stepping outside in August felt like being gently suffocated by a warm, well-meaning stranger. Charleston is a beautiful city. We just weren't built for it.

So in 2014 we moved to Asheville, which turned out to be the place we didn't know we were looking for. Cool enough in summer to sleep with the windows open. Close enough to the coast to visit when we want the ocean. Close enough to the mountains to be in them whenever the mood strikes, which in our case is often. A food scene that kept improving. A music scene that punched above its weight. Neighbors who had interesting things to say and didn't seem to mind that we were from somewhere else.

We are, without exaggeration, two of the luckiest people we know.

That's what this book has been trying to say, in the most roundabout way possible. Asheville is not perfect. No city is, and a city this conflicted about its own growth certainly isn't. The housing pressures are real. The post-Helene recovery is real and ongoing. The gap between what the region aspires to be and what it currently is remains wide enough to fall into.

And yet. The mountains are still there. The French Broad still runs, even when it runs too hard. The musicians still play on Friday nights, and the chefs still take risks that you wouldn't expect a city this size to support, and somewhere in these hills someone is building something that didn't exist before, the same as they always have.

The sarcasm in this book's title was, we hope, obvious from fairly early in chapter one. If it wasn't, consider this the admission. Don't move to Asheville was never the actual advice. It was a setup, and you were in on it, and the joke was always that Asheville is exactly the kind of place a book has to warn you away from in order to explain why you should go.

Don't move to Asheville. It's complicated, it's expensive, it's still recovering from a historic storm, and frankly the traffic on Merrimon Avenue has gotten completely out of hand.

Or move here. If you're like us, you'll love it.

225

A Note on the Machine Behind the Mountains

In the spirit of ruthless honesty, this book was written with the assistance of AI tools that helped with research, drafting, and organization. The concept, structure, editorial direction, and all final decisions were mine. I mention this not because I feel guilty, but because Asheville would never let me hear the end of it.

About the Author

Paul Wilczynski was born in Chicago, which should have been his first warning about weather. He survived it anyway, then spent nearly four decades in Boston, which is essentially Chicago but with worse drivers and a self-congratulatory accent. In 2008, having finally lost patience with winter, he moved to Charleston, South Carolina, where he discovered that escaping one kind of miserable climate is not the same as finding a good one.

Charleston was warm, which was the point. It was also approximately the surface temperature of the sun from May through September, with humidity that made the air feel less like something you breathe and more like something you wade through. He left in 2014. Asheville, it turned out, had figured out weather in a way that Boston and Charleston had conspicuously failed to do.

For most of his working life, Paul was a software developer, which means he spent decades persuading computers to do things they didn't want to do. This turned out to be excellent preparation for moving to Asheville, where the variables are endless, the outcomes are unpredictable, and the mountains make you forget you were trying to optimize anything. He lives in Asheville with his wife Joan and has no current plans to leave, which for him is something close to a miracle.

About the Designer

I couldn't be more thrilled with the incredible design Andrea Kulish Wilhelm poured into this book, but please don't hire her away from me. Andrea is a talented graphic design pro who does creative print design right here in Asheville's River Arts District. A first-generation Ukrainian American, she learned the traditional folk art of making pysanky eggs from her mother when she was only five. When she isn't bringing pages to life with her love for books and typography, she is busy spreading joy through her art. You can check out her work at Studio A or visit ashevillestudioa.com. Just don't take up too much of her time!

About the Type

Typeset in Plantin MT Pro, an old-style serif typeface. It was created in 1913 by the British Monotype Corporation for their hot metal typesetting system and is named after the sixteenth-century printer Christophe Plantin.